Distinctly Human

AND EVOLUTIONARY JOURNEY

Bruce Alpine

Distinctly Human
An Evolutionary Journey.
Bruce Alpine

Copyright © 2013 by Bruce H. Alpine

queries@brucealpine.com

Contact The Author:

Bruce-a@brucealpine.com

Book Layout © 2017 Bruce H. Alpine

Distinctly Human: An Evolutionary Journey.

ePub ISBN: 978-1-301-20346-8
Print ISBN: 978-1-542-35279-6

About The Author

Bruce Alpine is a science writer based out of the Kapiti Coast in New Zealand. Renowned for his ability to explain complex and technical issues in a way that is both easy to understand and fun to read, Bruce has gained a small but devoted audience since he published his first book, A History Of Life On Earth.

Born in Wellington, New Zealand in 1958, Bruce was the only son of a former college instructor. His mother was born in Britain and immigrated to New Zealand when she was 21. She encouraged Bruce and his three sisters to read often and study hard in school, and when it became clear that Bruce had an affinity for science, she encouraged that too.

Bruce's key interests revolve around the Earth and the life that inhabits it: how it sprang up, how it's come to be the way it is, how it functions now, etc. In addition to his work as a writer, Bruce is employed in the health support industry. He has two children, one son and one daughter, both of whom are grown up.

Contact The Author:

Bruce-a@brucealpine.com

Discover More Titles From Bruce Alpine:

https://brucealpine.com

Contents

Introduction

The evolution of man would have undoubtedly begun during the late Cretaceous period, 65 million years ago, the time the first Mammals appeared on Earth. The early mammals of the late cretaceous were small burrowing creatures, not unlike today's mice, others growing to a size comparable to modern domestic cats that were nocturnal in behaviour, to avoid the much larger Dinosaurs that were beginning to become extinct by the end of the Cretaceous period.

The mass extinction marking the end of the Dinosaur era was the beginning of the advance of mammals to the great apes, then ultimately, humans.

The earliest primate fossils appear in the Paleocene period, 55 million years ago. The Hominidae, or Great Apes, diverged from the Hylobatidae or ape family 15-20 million years ago. 14 million years ago, Orangutans evolved from the hominidae family. Early

hominid species, the Ardipithecus coming
around about 4-5 million years ago. The
chimpanzee and gorilla diverged at the same
time. Early hominids continued to diversify
into Ardipithecus then Australopithecus then
later the Homo genus.

During Charles Darwin's time, scientists believed early humans and apes evolved from
an early common ancestor. Independent
analysis during the twentieth century has
confirmed this with anatomical comparisons
between humans, chimpanzees, gorillas and
bonobos. The findings confirming, that humans and apes did indeed evolve from the
same early common ancestors as apes and
share much of their DNA.

Today, humans are still 98 percent chimpanzee. This does tend to lead to some confu-
sion however. Although humans and
chimpanzees do share certain DNA, humans
are not descendent from chimpanzees. But,
they do share an earlier common ancestor.

Less than 8 million years ago, a common
ancestor split into different lineages. Early
hominids and apes began their own independent diversification or changes, then
throughout the next 6 million years, continuing their own evolutionary process eventually becoming human and ape.

The most famous example of evidence supporting the divergence of human and ape from the earliest primates is the fossil record or skeletal remains. Bones, which have survived the test of time, displaying features which have helped define this evolutionary process. These fossilised remains are a snapshot in time, providing evidence and understanding of previous genera and species, throughout the evolutionary process of life. Evolutionary changes are still evident in and on the modern human body. Features that once in the Human history have had a definite useful purpose, but no longer have any significant use, for example:

- The Wisdom Teeth (Third Molars): Earlier in human evolution, humans needed an extra set of molars to make the mouth more productive with chewing raw meat, nuts, tubers and leaves, the body lacked the ability to sufficiently digest cellulose which made the extra set of molars particularly essential. Over time our dietary requirements changed, making our extra set of molars useless.

Evolution may be proving the uselessness of wisdom teeth, as thirty five percent of modern humans now do not grow their third molars. Indicating the wisdom teeth may be evolving out of existence

- Appendix: modern humans have absolutely no use for their Appendix. Most scientists agree with Charles Darwin's notion that the appendix was useful for processing cellulose, found in the earlier leaf rich diet. Over evolutionary changes, the appendix is likely to stay for a very long time, doing absolutely nothing.

- The Coccyx: commonly known as the Tailbone. A remnant of, the earlier tail. A tail was handy for gripping and swinging in trees. A tailbone has no such use in modern man.

- Goose Bumps: Modern humans get goose bumps when they are scared, cold or angry. Many animals also get goose bumps for the same reason, Goose bumps are what makes animal fur and hair stand on end when they are startled, cold or angry. When cold, it is this that creates warmth and insulation between the hairs.

Handy in the early human evolutionary process when humans wore no clothes and instead had a natural fur coat, but no particular purpose in modern humans.

In my earlier book A History Of Life On Earth. I outlined the divergence between living forms of life on Earth. In this book, I will outline the divergence or the evolutionary process from our common ancestor to modern man. As was the case in A History Of Life On Earth, I will also present the scientific evidence, which supports the evolutionary process from the same common ancestor of apes through the geological periods to modern humans.

Despite the tiresome, bitter tirades from creationists and critics alike, Paleoanthropologists have identified many evolutionary transitions from a common ancestor of apes leading up to modern ape and human. From Ardipithecus and Australopithecus, who had different features to modern man, they held similarities to an early human ancestor. From Australopithecus to the Various Homo variants, again, there are features similar to apes more than modern man. But, then again, they share many common features with modern man. From the earliest Homo to the Homo sapiens, the common features are becoming more and more similar to modern man than ape. But these similarities at no time suggest that modern man is not another Ape species.

Human Evolution

Evolution is the study of common ancestor origination on earth 3.7 billion years ago and leading to an explanation of all life on Earth.

Human evolution is the study of common hominid ancestors originating in Africa and the lengthy process of change leading up to modern human.

I could simply claim we are all here because evolution did it. I could write a book claiming that evolution is the almighty power that created everything, including us. That everyone should live their lives and interact according to evolution, as if evolution is a form of deity. And, who could question it? After all, it is written in this book. I could model the book on Evolutionary law. Such a book sounds preposterous doesn't it? As is with any book that claims some deity made everything including us.

Actually, Evolutionary law is the reason we are all here, Evolutionary law is a natural law. It is the slow, lengthy process that has taken place over the last 3.7 billion years since life first appeared on earth as simple organisms, leading to all forms of life either now extinct or surviving on earth today, including us.

Either as criticism or a total lack of understanding, some groups of people, mainly creationists, following religious doctrine claim that the 19th century naturalist Charles Darwin claims that humans evolved from apes in his top selling publication On The Origin Of species (1859) Darwin actually

never mentions humans in his book, except
for the third paragraph from the end, when
Darwin writes:

*"In the distant future, light will be thrown on
the origin of man and his history"*.

In his later book however, The Descent Of
Man. (1871) Darwin teasingly mentions humans evolving from apes as this followed a
popular belief during the 19th century. Now
in the twenty first century, we know that
statement to be not, well, completely true.
We now know that modern man and modern
ape evolved from a common ancestor.

Jean-Baptiste Lamarck (1744-1829) seems to
be the first to propose that human evolved
from apes. In his daring for his time publication Philosophie zoologique (1809):

"Certainly, if some race of apes, especially
the most perfect among them, lost, by neces-
sity of circumstances, or some other cause,
the habit of climbing trees and grasping
branches with the feet and if the individuals
of that race, over generations, were forced to
use their feet only for walking and ceased to
use their hands as feet, doubtless … these
apes would be transformed into two-handed
beings and … their feet would no longer
serve any purpose other than to walk."

Other Naturalists adopted the notion that humans evolved from apes. Scottish geologist, Robert Chambers (1802-1871) in his Vestiges of the natural history of Creation, Chambers stated that the apes are distinguished by:

"Greater relative magnitude of brain, by agility, and by the use of the hand. The signal superiority of the human species is thus prepared for and betokened in the immediately preceding portions of the line: it might have been seen, ere man existed, that a remarkable creature was coming upon the earth."

Charles Darwin was the first to propose that small changes over billions of years has resulted in the species we see today, through a process of natural selection, or the survival of the fittest. Darwin based his theory of evolution on observations he had made around the World on a scientific expedition onboard the survey ship HMS Beagle, during the early 1830's. Darwin realised that species evolved and then became extinct, others have diversified and survived until modern day. Since Darwin's time, many early hominids have come to light through fossil records that confirms 19th century beliefs that Modern Man did indeed evolve from a common ancestor, as did apes.

Human evolution are changes over a lengthy process by which modern humans originated from common ancestors of apes, evolving over a period of approximately 6 million years. The most major change was the ability of Bipedalism, or the ability to walk upright on two legs, which evolved over four million years. Another major change was a larger more complex brain. The ability to make and use tools, also the ability for language, which developed over the last one hundred thousand years.

Humans are primates, many scientists today, including British evolutionary biologist Richard Dawkins refers to modern humans as, The Fifth Ape. Modern humans, Homo sapiens have very similar characteristics to the ape. Chimpanzees and humans share a common ancestor that lived 6-8 million years ago in the continent of Africa. Much of the human evolution occurred in Africa. The fossil evidence on humans who lived 2-6 million years ago, are discovered entirely in Africa.

Throughout this book, you will read about scientists who discovered fossil remains of early hominids, who hold the title of paleoanthropologist and anthropologist. I will explain those fields:

- Anthropology: is the study of biology, culture and society. The field involves understanding differences and similarities between species and humans in the genes (DNA), physiology and behaviour.

- Paleoanthropology: is a subfield of anthropology and is the study of human evolution. Paleoanthropologists search for the roots of human physical traits and behaviour, the endeavour to find out how evolution has shaped the potentials, tendencies and limitations of all people.

My father used to say that, through culture,
humans effectively domesticated themselves.

—Richard E. Leakey

CHAPTER ONE

Early Primates

P rimates are remarkably new to the evolutionary time scale. The earth has existed for 4.5 billion years. But, life has only existed for the last 3.6 billion years. The first primates did not appear until around 65 million years ago, before the end of the Cretaceous period. The end of the Cretaceous saw the extinction of the Dinosaur. At this time, the earth was very different from today as the super-continent of

Pangaea was breaking apart and slowly forming the continents that we are familiar with today. Towards the end of the Cretaceous, Europe was still attached to North America. North America had not yet connected to South America. Modern Asia was also not yet connected to India. Most landmasses were warm and tropical, except for Australia, which was still over Antarctica. Large reptiles were slowly being taken over by small furry mammals. After the major extinction event at the end of the cretaceous, the small, furry mammals were being replaced by, larger mammals.

The landscape would have looked very different from today as grasses had not yet evolved along with most modern plant and tree life we see in today's world. Common domestic animals such as sheep, cattle and wildebeests are absent, until the diversification of grass. Some marsupials, such as opossum like mammals are appearing to occupy the large forested areas. The earth is devoid of flowering plants. Forests of broadleafed trees are developing over much of earth's landscape.

Proto-Primates

After the major dramatic extinction event, which marked the end of the Cretaceous period and the demise of the Dinosaur, 65 million years ago, the first primates appeared in northern Africa. Proto-primates at this time were around the same size of Squirrels and tree Shrews of today. Fragmentary fossil evidence suggesting they were adapted for life in very warm, moist climates. Their feet were padded and clawed for climbing trees in the heavily forested areas, they would have been faster moving on the ground rather than in trees, their hands had grasping digits adapted for prolonged periods in trees, eating mainly berries and leaves. Their eyesight would have been relatively good.

Around 40 million years ago, earliest primates began living in groups. At this time, they also developed the wet nose, which is common among land based Mammals of today. Modern examples are the lemurs, Simian monkeys, tarsiers and apes. Protoprimates at this time lost the bodily ability to produce vitamin C, instead becoming reliant on external sources of vitamin C by eating berries and fruits to compliment their leaf diet.

30 million years ago, as Africa was becoming increasingly separated with the continental drift, primates remained in Africa. Some may have migrated to south America as at this time, south America was beginning its drift towards the modern day north America. Only a narrow sea separated Africa from South America, travel would have been possible on drifting logs. Found in north and west Africa, north and south America, the Arabian Peninsula and South Asia are Oligo-

cene fossil deposits containing primate bones dating back 30-40 five million years, suggesting primates were about the size of a large squirrel and some, the size of a large domestic Cat. North America and Europe had drifted far enough apart to become distinct continents of their own. The Great Rift Valley in North east Africa was formed at this time The Great Rift Valley is today a valuable site for modern fossil evidence, containing evidence supporting the evolutionary process of the very earliest human like creatures, which I will investigate in more detail in the next chapter.

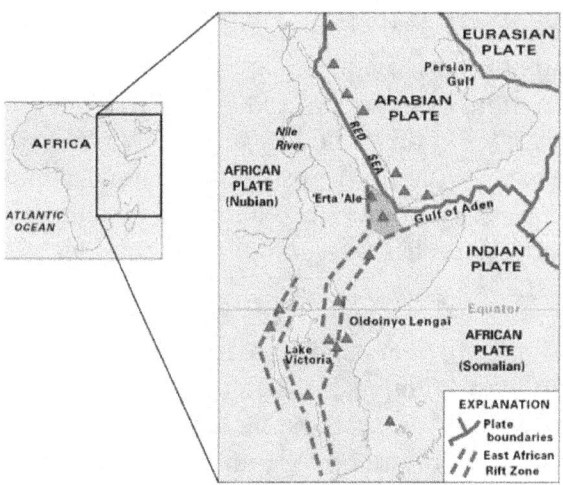

The Great Rift Valley in dotted lines.

Polar ice caps were forming at the north and south Poles, causing a sea level drop. In turn greatly increasing the distance between continental land-masses and changing the earths climate. However, the global climate was warmer than today.

25 million years ago, proto primates split into two separate Evolutionary lineages. One would eventually diversify into modern monkeys. The other will eventually diversify or evolve into modern man or the early Hominid and the modern apes. Primate fossils are very commonly dating back to this time in the evolutionary process, especially for apes. Not all primates however are equally represented in the fossil record. Monkeys are comparatively rare.

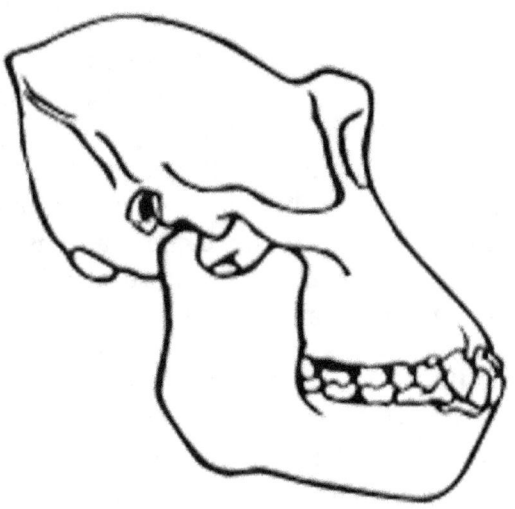

A Modern Gorilla cranium

About 10 million years ago, the early hominid separated from the lineage of the modern gorilla. Ancestors to modern man are begin-

ning to adapt to life on the edge of expansive
Savannahs of southern Europe as grass species appear on the earths landscape. Pre humans at this time were living primarily in
savannahs. The large grassy areas dotted
with shrubs and trees would become usual
habitat for pre human and future human species, including the earliest species of early
human, Ardipithecus and Australopithecus.
The tall grass of the savannahs encouraged
pre human primates to stand upright.

Around nine million years ago, cooler, less
hospitable climatic conditions caused the
extinction of a great number of these primates, except for some who managed to migrate south into Africa and south Asia.
Cooler climatic conditions were caused from
the continued formation of ice caps at the
poles and the continued continental drifts,
which were forming high mountainous areas,
were changing the global weather patterns.
Alpine glaciers were forming in some of
these mountainous areas.

Eight million years ago grasses had evolved
and challenged the land areas previously
dominated by forests. Grasses began a land
grab, taking land away from trees and re-
stricting forests to smaller areas with grassy
savannahs in between.

Six million years ago, grasses dominated the
land, allowing the evolution of mammals to
diversify and take advantage of grassy envi-

ronments. At the same time abandoning the forests for the more vast, open areas of the savannahs. Some animals diversifying and developing multiple stomachs better adapted for the digestion of grass.

Early hominids also took advantage of grassy savannahs around five million years ago. Developing bipedalism or the ability to stand on two feet, developing the ability to walk upright. Eventually shaping our earliest ancestors into the species that became Homo sapiens.

One species of grass has been extremely beneficial and nurtured early humans over the last ten thousand years, wheat. Allowing humans to grow in communities after the invention of farming to sustain ever growing towns and cities that today dominate the landscape of today's earth.

Seven million years ago, hominid separated from the evolutionary lineage from our most common ancestor, the chimpanzee. Chimpanzees and humans both have a Larynx that repositions during the first two years after birth to a spot towards the front of the lower half of the throat, the pre-curser to speech.

Within the next two million years, the differences between early humans and the chimpanzee would finally become quite distinct.

Sahelanthropus tchadensis

Dating back seven million years the Sahelan-
thropus is widely believed the first species
which is modern mans earliest ancestor and
the earliest ancestor to modern chimpanzees
or the earliest human-chimpanzee divergence, before Human ancestor and chimpanzee ancestor split from the lineage to
eventually become modern chimpanzee and
modern man. Nicknamed Toumai meaning
Hope of Life in the Dazaga language of
Chad in central Africa and are member of the
Great Ape grouping, which include chimpanzees, gorillas, humans and orangutans.
Fossil evidence consists of jaw and some
teeth that have a mix of derived and primitive features. Facial features differ markedly
from early human species. Cranial features
show a flat face, small front teeth as compared to other members of the ape grouping
and heavy brow ridges or ridges above the
eyes.

The existing fossils were discovered in the
Djurab desert in Chad by a team led by paleoanthropologist Michel Brunet of the College de France. All specimens were
discovered between July 2001 and March
2002

This was maybe the first ape-like species to
be bipedal, or the ability to walk on two feet
and stand upright. The evidence is a hole at
the bottom of the skull, where the spinal col-

umn meets the skull. This hole or opening is toward the middle of the skull. If the hole were towards the back of the skull, this would provide evidence the species stood of all four legs.

Orrorin tugenensis

The first Orrorin tugenensis fossils were discovered in 2001 in the Lukeino Formation, near lake Baringo in western Kenya. Fossilised remains include lower jaw and teeth, arm and thigh bones. Iindicating this creature lived between 6 million, 100 thousand years ago till 5 million, 800 thousand years ago, they were discovered by anthropologists. Brigitte Senut and Martin Pickford of the Museum national d'Histoire naturelle in the Tugen Hills region in Kenya. Tugenensis is the only member so far of the Orrorin species to be discovered and is the earliest human of the evolutionary tree because of its novel combination of ape and Modern human features. Orrorin turgenensis could be the fabled and proverbial 'Missing link" between apes and humans.

Orrorin tugenensis was bipedal and able to stand upright, also adapted to climb trees. The limb bones suggest this species was about the same size as a chimpanzee and is a direct descendant of modern humans. The size of the brain is unknown as no cranial or skull evidence has yet been discovered making estimates of the brain cavity size impossible and cannot be measured.

Existing fossils of other organisms in the Lake Baringo region indicates this species lived in a dry evergreen forested area, which suggests it probably had the same diet as modern day Ape which includes leaves, fruit, seeds, roots, nuts and insects.

CHAPTER TWO

Ardipithecus

Appearing on earth around one million years after the common ancestor of apes split from the same lineage. Ardipithecus presented a strange mix of chimp and human-like features. Ardipithecus was the first genus to walk on both feet, although, no where near as adept as the following Australopithecus genus. Ardipithecus brain was unusually small as compared to the brain of the Australopithecus, which would evolve in another half a million years, his brain has more in common with a chimps brain.

In comparison with chimpanzee, where males fight one another for dominance regularly, Ardipithecus seem to be a more sedate genus with no apparent evidence of male to male fighting or conflict for domination, to attract a female and to repel a male from another pack. A chimpanzee male has larger, more menacing teeth than the female. Ardipithecus however have similar sized teeth between male and female, suggesting an aggression free, placid existence.

Existing evidence for the Ardipithecus suggests they habited woodlands and the savannah plains of Africa.

Species for the Ardipithecus genus are consisted of Ardipithecus ramidus and Ardipthecus kadabba.

Ardipithecus is a fossil homonoid, representing the very first hominid. Two sub-species are represented in the Ardipithecus genus, the ramidus and the kadabba sub-species. The first Ardipithecus fossil was discovered in September 1994, that being the ramidus subspecies. The name, Ardipithecus comes from the Afar language, in which Ardi means ground/floor and Pithecus, which comes from the Greek word meaning monkey.

Until 1994, scientists believed the first example of a true human ancestor was the Australopithecus, for which previous fossil skeletal remains belonging to the famous Lucy, which were discovered in 1974, dating back around three million years.

Ardipithecus ramidus

Between 1992 and 1994, a team of paleoanthropologists, led by Tim White from the American University of California at Berkeley, discovered skeletal remains from a previously unknown species of true human ancestor, he later called Ardipithecus ramidus dating back 4.5 million years, ramidus, coming from the Arabic word ramid, meaning, root.

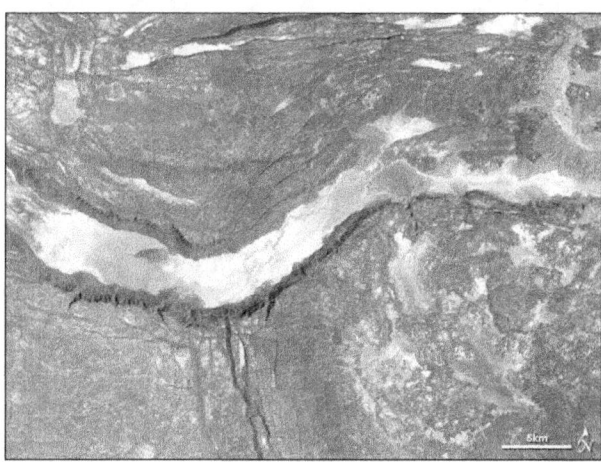

Satellite image of the Awash region of East Africa Rift

Since the initial discovery White has found over one hundred fossil specimens of the

Ardipithecus ramidus equating to 45 percent of a full skeleton and affectionately named his specimens Ardi. His discovery in the Middle Awash area of Ethiopia is a region of the Great Rift Valley of North east Africa.

The Great Rift Valley, is preferred to be called East Africa Rift today. The rift, a geographic trench extends 6000 kilometres or 3,700 miles between South east Asia and extends to south east Mozambique in south east Africa. The East Africa Rift is an area of tectonic plates, which is continually trying to create new plates, in the process it is continually bringing ancient fossils to the surface. The Rift is referred to as one of the geologic wonders of the world. The most refined finds are in the Awash region of Ethiopia.

Fossil evidence for Ardipithecus ramidus suggests it had a grasping big toe for ease of movement in trees. Other features suggest it was also adapted for movement on the ground as well with smaller canine teeth, these teeth suggest the main diet would have been non abrasive food such as berries, fruit with some meat as the enamel around the teeth is thin. If the enamel were thicker, this would suggest that Ardipithecus ate more abrasive food such as nuts and tubers.

Ardipithecus tooth enamel in thickness are slightly thicker than that of a chimpanzee and slightly thinner than that of the later Australopithecus suggesting a mixed diet.

Ardipithecus ramidus adults were about three feet, eleven inches or one hundred and twenty centimetres tall, with no apparent difference between male and female, suggesting that male Ardipithecus did not have to compete against one another to gain dominance. Ardipithecus ramidus show some similarities to apes and ape traits with its lager toe for moving around in trees with a shorter, broader pelvis than an apes.

The brain size for the Ardipithecus ramidus is rather small. Smaller when comparing it with a chimpanzee and considerably smaller than that of a gorilla. Smaller also than that of the later Australopithecus and about a quarter than the size of a modern human brain.

Once the lineages between chimpanzee and humans separated, both underwent substantial changes in the evolutionary process. Chimpanzee feet are more adapted for climbing trees and the Ardipithecus is more adapted to moving on the ground rather than trees. Male and female Ardipithecus are similar in size, indicating between male and Female, there were most probably no hierarchy system and no male to male conflict, which is in contrast to chimpanzees where male to male conflicts are common and essential for a social structure

Ardipithecus Kadabba

First discovered in 1997 in the Middle Awash region in Ethiopia. Ardipithecus kadabba gets its name from kadabba, meaning oldest ancestor

In 2004, while studying the skeletal remains of Ardipithecus ramidus he had previously discovered in 1996 with Paleoanthropologist Tim White, Paleontologist Yoahannes Haile-Selassie of Cleveland Museum Of Natural History, noticed some teeth and pieces of bone indicating another subspecies of Ardipithecus, as the teeth were showing signs of a different wear pattern.

The teeth structure was closer resembling that of the chimpanzee. He believed this new species height would be closer to that of a chimpanzee. He dated these teeth as 5.5 million years old, a full million years older than his previously discovered Ardipithecus ramidus. He named this subspecies Ardipithecus kadabba.

The back teeth of the Ardipithecus kadabba are larger than a Chimpanzee. Its front teeth are smaller, indicating this species ate mainly abrasive fibrous food such as nuts. The larger back teeth indicates it would have done most of its chewing at the back of the mouth.

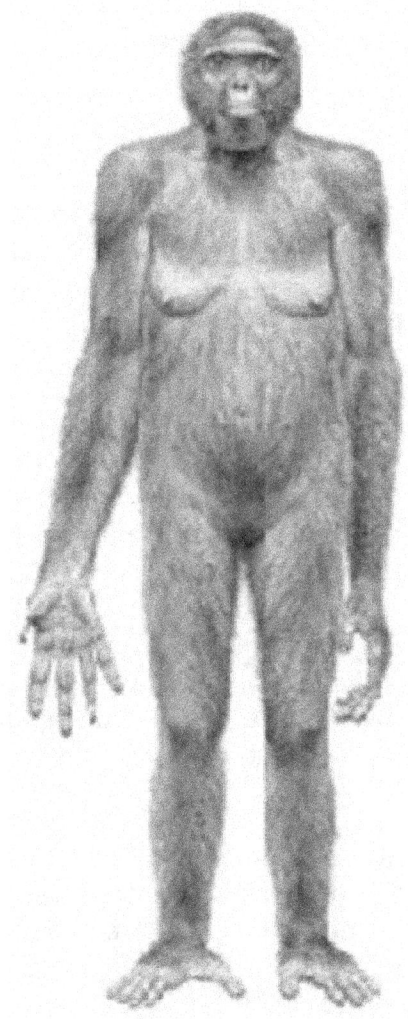

Ardipithecus ramidus

This species is only known from a small
number of bones, mainly jaw and cranium
fragments. The evidence is clear that

Ardipithecus kadabba had a brain the same size as a modern chimpanzee

Although Ardipithecus is the first known hominid, descendent from a common ancestor of the chimpanzee and other apes. Ardipithecus was about the same size as a chimp but did not look or act in the same way. Ardipithecus was an adept tree climber. Also, walking upright on the ground in and around semi-arid woodland areas and also in grassy savannahs. Early hominids became upright in response to living in these areas.

In some ways Ardipithecus was less advanced than chimpanzees, Chimpanzees had long strong arms and hands. Their fingers were curved and grasping feet to climb trees, swing through the branches. Feeding while hanging in the trees. Ardipithecus lacked those features. Instead, it walked atop the tree branches, in much the same way as monkeys do today.

It is not known what the walking motion of the Ardipithecus looked like, but its almost certain that they would have taken shorter less efficient steps than humans do today because the bigger toe off to the side as opposed to inline with the other toes would have been partially problematic. Prohibiting them from taking great strides. The big toe would have certainly aided tree climbing in the way Gorillas and Chimps

CHAPTER THREE

Australopithecus

A ustralopithecus gets its name from the Latin word, Australis, meaning southern and the Greek word pithe- kos, meaning ape. Australopithecus is a genus of early hominid, which evolved in eastern Africa around four million years ago, then spreading throughout the African conti- nent within another two million years.

Australopithecus played a significant role in the human evolutionary process, eventually evolving into the homo genus in Africa around two million years ago.

A gracious genus, Australopithecus shared numerous traits with apes and Humans, providing a constant rate of evolution and were relatively widespread throughout the African continent, especially northern and eastern Africa by three and a half million years ago. Footprints can be observed in Tanzania, on a site called Laetoli. Containing prints that are remarkably similar to those of modern humans and have been dated to three to four million years ago. These footprints have been attributed to Australopithecus, because this is the only pre-human to have existed at this time.

The first Australopithecus to be discovered was the fossil of a three year old in a lime quarry of an Australopithecus africanus by a group of workers in Taung, South Africa. This specimen was studied by Raymond Dart, an Australian anatomist working at the University of Witwatersrand in Johannesburg. Dart realized the fossil contained a number of human features which suggested it was an early Human ancestor in 1925. Dart and Scottish paleoanthropologist Robert Broom ten years later set about finding more specimens in numerous other sites and found a Australopithecus Africanus along with other specimens Broom has called Paranthrobus robustus. There is still very much debate from anthropologists if Paranthrobus

robustus belong to the australopithecus genus or should be categorized as another genus. At this point in time, P rubustus is still
categorized as a species of Australopithecus.

An excavation in 1959 in the Olduvai Gorge
in Tanzania, Eastern Africa revealed the
skull belonging to an Australopithecus boisei
by Mary Leakey. Since then, the Leakey
family has continued to excavate the Olduvai
Gorge, finding many other specimens, including Homo habilis and Homo erectus.

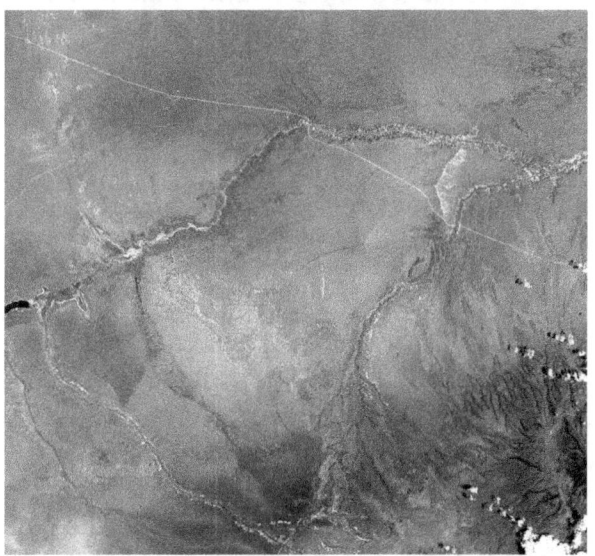

Satellite image of the Olduvai Gorge in Tanzania

Recently the fossils of Australopithecus
sediba, which lived two million years ago,
have been discovered in Malapa Cave in
South Africa, giving some scientists the no-

tion that the Australopithecus sediba eventually evolved into Homo erectus.

Australopithecus afarensis

Discovered in northern Africa, Laetoli being the most significant site, extensive fossilised remains have been found in Hadar, Afar region of Ethiopia, including the more famous specimen, Lucy. Other sites include Kenya and koobi. Paleoanthropologists have recovered over three hundred individuals. This species managed to survive for nine hundred thousand years, which is four times as long as the modern humans have survived on earth.

Australopithecus afarensis is believed to have lived three to four million years ago and is most closely related to the

Homo genus for which humans belong to the Homo sapien genus, an American paleoanthropologist, Donald Johanson and colleagues when discovering the earliest specimen of the Australopithecus afarensis in 1974 continually played the Beatles song Lucy In The Sky With Diamonds decided on the name for their most famous find, Lucy in the Afar Triangle region of Hadar in Ethiopia. Some specimens of afarensis previously found in the 1930s have been incorporated into the fossil collection for Australopithecus afarensis.

Compared to Great Apes, Australopithecus afarensis has reduced teeth. Although they are still larger than modern humans, their jaws are forward projecting as compared to humans. They also have a relatively smaller brain than modern humans. A primitive hominid with a small brain and primitive face was contrary to an earlier belief that an increased brain size was the first major adaptive shift for hominids. Before the 1970s it was widely believed that a larger brain was responsible for the upright standing in early Hominids.

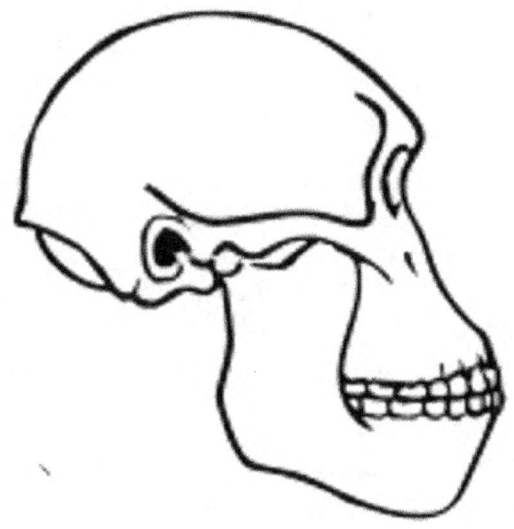

Australopithecus Skull

There is great continuing debate around the ease of movement of the Australopithecus afarensis. The lack of the big toe evident in earlier pre-human species is lacking in the fossil remains.Indicating the Australopithecus was more adapted to moving on the ground as opposed to a mix of walking on the ground and climbing trees, a larger toe is still present but is smaller and more inline with the other toes on each foot. Allowing for more ease of movement than previous species of hominid. Arched feet and a lumbar arch apparent in the fossil record, suggests this species walked with increased ease. The pelvis is more human like as opposed to ape like. The hips are short and wide, suggesting the Australopithecus afarensis was slender in build, which gives for thought that this species was far more adapted to walking upright.

Computer simulations, using inertial properties and Kinematics suggest that Australopithecus afarensis was able to move and walk around in the same way as modern humans. Though longer arms do suggest that some tree climbing may have been part of life.

The Social Characteristics of Australopithecus afarensis is not well known but the difference in body size between male and female suggests that males were relatively larger than females. Males were on average four foot eleven inches or one hundred and fifty one centimetres, Females were on average three feet, five inches or one hundred and five centimeters. Comparing this with other known great ape species suggests that a social group would have been small and consists of a dominant male and a number of breeding females.

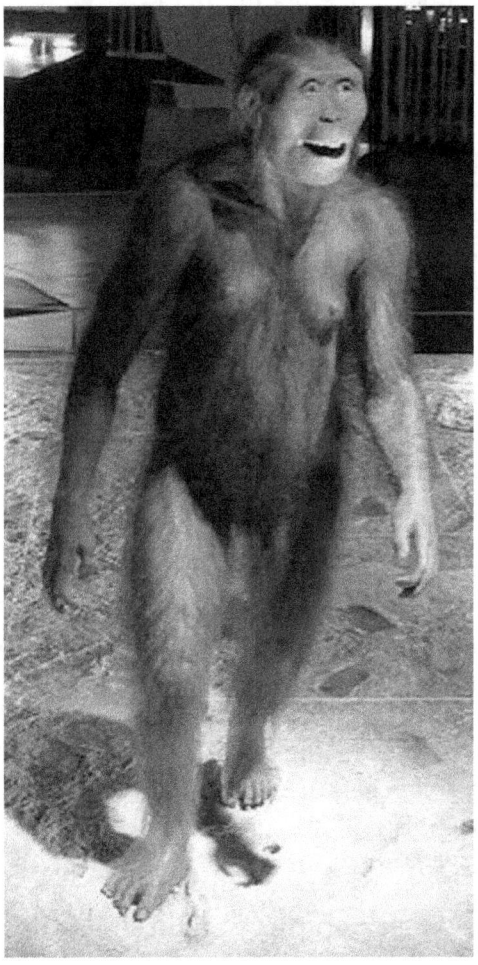

Reconstruction of an Australopithecus afarensis

A characteristic similar to chimpanzees is that children grew more rapidly and reached adulthood far earlier than modern humans do today, leaving less time for parental guidance and socializing during childhood. Australopithecus ate mainly plant-based foods including seeds, nuts, roots, leaves, fruit and small Lizards

The continued ability to walk upright was by far the most important feature of evolution toward modern man, Australopithecus afarensis were quite adept at bipedalism. This ability grew more important as the savannahs grew as the forests retreated in Africa, though A.afarensis would not have spent much time on the ground as they are vilnerable to large predators, they would not have had any protection from leopards or large sabre toothed cats

In 2010, a study published in the Nature Journal suggested that Australopithecus ate and carved meat from animal carcasses with stone tools, which threw back a long held belief that hominids did not use such tools before two and a half million years ago. This study suggests early hominids were using stone tools and implements three and a half million years ago.

Australopithecus bahrelghazali

Paleoanthropologist Michel brunet of the College de France in 1993, discovered the fossilised remains of skull fragments and lower jaw of the Australopithecus bahrel-ghazali. He effectionately named this specimen Abel, so named after a Brunet's deceased colleague Abel Brillanceau. Brunet discovered the remains west of the east African Great Rift Valley, in Chad.

The teeth contained in the lower jaw are consistent with the Australopithecus afarensis and has been dated to 3.5 million years ago. Again, the same range as the Australopithecus afarensis. By 1996, Brunet classified the specimen as Australopithecus bahrel-ghazali.

This species is another mystery, as it seems to be the only Australopithecus species found in Central Africa.

Australopithecus africanus

Africa is the home of the great apes. Charles Darwin strongly believed Africa was also the cradle for humanity, from where all humans of the world originated from. He knew that eventually evidence would turn up. Darwin knew that it would only take someone who was able to recognise it when it did.

In 1924, 31 year old Australian doctor, Raymond Dart arrived in an area of south Africa to begin a teaching career where no one had previously thought or cared about looking for evidence of human ancestry, Johannesburg, south Africa.

On October 24, Dart received news of a
spectacular find by colleagues and students
of fossilised remains in a nearby lime stone
quarry. Among the chest of remains was a
fossilised brain cavity, which Dart recognised was considerably larger than that of a
typical chimpanzee. Yet, the cavity was not
big enough to belong to any previously
known primitive man. Further inspection he
found the upper jaw. He realised the brain
and jaw belonged to the same person and had
been sent the fossilised remains of an ancient
ape-man and thought it could be the missing
link between ape and man.

Over several weeks of chipping away at the
fossilised rock, Dart realised he had uncov-
ered something extraordinary. The face of a
child with both ape and human, features
which had never been discovered before.
One fascinating feature was a skull showing
the Foramen magnum or a hole at the base of
the skull, which connects the spinal cord to
the base of the skull. Allowing for upright
posture. More like human posture than Australopithecus afarensis. Dart named the
specimen after the name of the lime quarry
the fossil was found in, Taung and named
the specimen, Taung child, or Australopithecus africanus or, the southern ape of Africa.
Dating back in the human evolutionary time
line at over two million years. Placing the
human ancestry firmly in Africa for the first
time and was more apelike than anyone previously had imagined.

The first molar teeth were just beginning to erupt through the gum of the Taung Child, indicating the teeth definitely did belong to a child. Further investigation of the fossilised jaw indicated the child was three years old at the time of death. At three years old, Taung child is comparative to the size of an eighteen months old modern child.

Compared to Australopithecus afarensis, africanus has a more rounded cranium or skull housing a larger brain and smaller teeth. With other ape like features, such as long arms and a strong sloping face that extends out from under the brain cavity with a pronounced jaw.

Available fossil evidence suggests that Australopithecus males were taller than females. Males average about four feet, six inches or one hundred and thirty eight centimeters and females on average were three feet nine inches or one hundred and fifteen centimeters.

South Africa, two million years ago was a place similar to the savannah today, was a place where food was scarce and predators such as sabre toothed cats, giant hyennas along with a large varying array of large animals that have since become extinct on the face of the earth, were never too far away. Australopithecus africanus would have scavenged their food mainly from kills made by these predators. Life for these early

humans would have been extremely dangerous, as predators would also have preyed on
Australopithecus africanus. Taungs mother
would have used stone implements to break
open bone for its rich bone marrow protein.

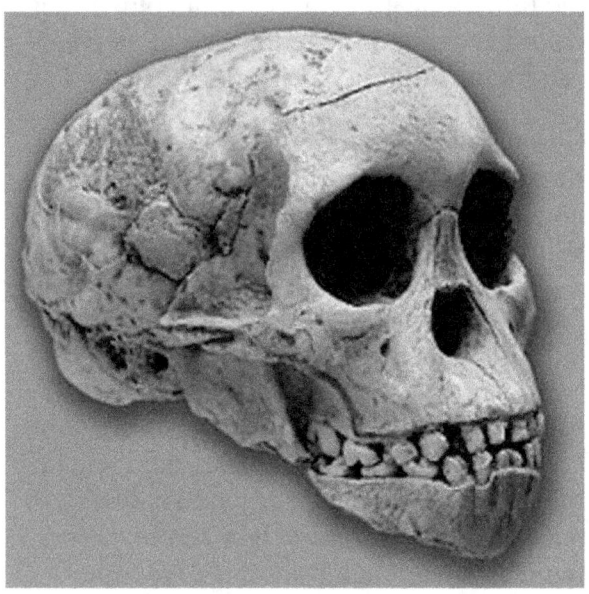

Reconstruction of Taung Child's Skull

Taung child's skull was discovered in fossilised stone along with egg remains and other
broken skulls, typical to deposits found in
Eagles nests. Eagles today have huge weight
to lift ratios that can carry relatively large
objects. The skull also reveals scratching
typically from a large beak, poking to access
the nutrient rich brain matter of its prey.

During the 1940s and 1950s Dart discovered
fossils along with broken animal bones.

Which, Dart assumed meant that the Australopithecus africanus were hunters who used
these bones as a weapon for hunting. During
the 1970s and 1980s other scientists realised
these bones belonged to prey of predators,
such as lions, leopards and hyenas, who also
ate Australopithecus africanus individuals as
well.

Tooth wear, size and shape can all give clues
to what a certain species consumed. Scientists have determined the Australopithecus
africanus consumed abrasive foods, consist-
ing of meat, nuts as well as a diet of softer
foods such as fruits and plants.

As I mentioned earlier Australopithecus,
were sometimes eaten by predators. Australopithecus species including africanus would
have lived together in groups for protection,
as nighttime in Africa was a dangerous
place. Early hominids would have been very
vulnerable to predators.

At the time of the Australopithecus africanus, the African landscape was changing
dramatically and the global climate was
changing around three million years ago.
This change was not due to the early habi-
tants, volcanic activity or any asteroid im-
pact. Rather the cause was in space. The
earth orbit with the sun is elliptical. An elliptical orbit allows for periodic changes. Three
million years ago, this orbit changed, which
caused the earth to point away from the sun,

plunging the northern hemisphere into an ice age. As the glaciers advanced in the north, the geography in the south changed as well. In Africa this change caused some forest to retreat, opening up vast savannahs. As the glaciers also locked up moisture, the environment in Africa also became drier, destroying large areas of wetland where previous early hominids had inhabited. As a result, Africa became warmer and drier.

Australopithecus garhi

In 1996, the Australopithecus garhi was believed to be the final missing link between the Australopithecus genus and the homo genus, until 2008, when a young boy found the first fossil of the Australopithecus sebida. More about that in the next section.

A research team led by an Ethiopian paleontologist Berhane Asfew and the American paleoanthropologist Tim White discovered this species in the Middle Awash of Ethiopia's Afar depression in 1996. The species has been dated as 2.5 million years old. This species was confirmed as a new species of the Australopithecus genus in November 1997. Garhi means, Surprise in the local Afar language.

Australopithecus garhi is not very well documented. Fossil remains discovered so far consists of cranial or the top of the head and other fragmented skeletal specimens. It is is believed how-ever that this species had a longer femur or upper leg bone, allowing for longer strides in motion than previous Australopithecus species.

Fossil evidence of the Australopithecus garhi seems to be associated with the first known stone tools along with animal bones that appear to have been cut and broken open to expose bone marrow with those stone tools. For a long time anthropologists believed it were early homo who produced stone tools. In Ethiopia approximately three thousand stone artifacts have been found, dating to an estimated two and a half million year of age. It is highly probable that the Australopithecus garhi was the first to transition to stone tool making in order to break animal bones and change to the highly nutritious diet that pumped the evolutionary process.

Australopithecus sediba

In August 2008, two partial skeletons were discovered close together amongst sedimentary cave deposits at the Malapa site at the Cradle Of Humankind World Heritage Site in South Africa. These fossils represent a new species of Australopithecus and probably descended from Australopithecus africanus. They are aged at one million nine hundred and fifty thousand years to one million, seven hundred and eighty thousand years old.

The first of the finds were discovered by nine years old Matthew Berger, while walking around and exploring near his Fathers excavation site in the dolomite hills of Johannesburg, on the Malapa Nature reserve. He suddenly noticed a fossilised bone protruding out of the ground. He could not believe what he had found and alerted his dad who is paleoanthropologist Lee R. Berger from the University of the Witwatersrand. His father was amased at his sons find. On further observation, the fossilised rock had a jaw and a tooth sticking our. The fossil turned out to belong to a Four foot, two inch or one point twenty seven metre juvenile male. The actual skull of this individual was later discovered on March 2010 by Berger's team. Berger's team also found skeletal remains of saber-toothed cats, mongooses and antelopes. Berger and his team speculated they may have all fallen into a deep hole by the lure of the scent of water and remained in the cave until being buried by water and sand. Fossilising to preserve the remains.

A range of features of the Australopithecus sediba suggests this is a transitional species between the Australopithecus species and the Homo species. The cranial capacity or the brain capacity is that of 95 percent adult and is of a higher range from Australopithecus africanus. But, lower than the lower range of the early Homo. The tooth size is similar to that of the Homo erectus. So similar that if found without other species earlier, this could easily be mistaken for Homo erectus. However, the tooth spacing is more similar to the Australopithecus species. It certainly seems at this stage that Australopithecus is a direct ancestor to early homo.

Australopithecus sediba's hands are surprisingly modern. Its precision grip suggests it was also an early tool making Australopithecus.

Kenyanthropus

Kenyanthrobus platyops, dates back around 3.5 million years to 3 million years ago. A hominid fossil discovered in Lake Turkana in Kenya in 1999 by Justus Erus, a research assistant working with Meave Leakey. Leakey in 2001 proposed that the fossil represents a new genus. This causes some controversy as others propose that it is an individual belonging to Australopithecus afarensis. Which is known to have existed at this time in the same geographic area.

Meave Leakey named Kenyanthropus platyops, meaning Flat Face Man Of Kenya, as it appears to be the only species in its genus. Features belonging to the fossil give it a broad flat face, allowing some paleoanthropologists to believe it actually belongs to the Homo genus, perhaps being a, direct ancestor. Teeth are typically human and also typically ape with a toe that suggests it probably walked upright. Until the controversy is settled, the fossilised remains will remain a mystery.

Satellite image of Lake Turkana in Kenya

Until recently it was believed that Australopithecus afarensis was the last ancestor to the Homo genus. This species was made famous with the fossil remains of Lucy, It appears that Lucy may have shared the grassy savannahs of Africa with a rival.

Kenyanthropus has small ear holes, similar to that of chimpanzees and also shares many features with primitive hominids for instance, a small brain. Some striking differences are high cheek bones. Below its nose bone is a flat plane, giving it a flat face.

Future fossil discoveries may provide further information and hopefully enlighten the existence of Kenyanthropus, so its species and genus can be confirmed and placed in its rightful place in the evolution of the Human species. This species may be proof there were two different human ancestors existing at the same time.

CHAPTER FOUR

Paranthropus

Paranthropus, taken from the Greek words Para, meaning beside and anthropus meaning Human consists of three sub-species, the Paranthropus aethiopicus, Paranthropus boisei and Paranthropus robustus. Until recently, these three species were considered sub-species of the earlier Australopithecus genus. Some scientists, in particular Robert Broom and Bernard

Wood suggest there are differences between Australopithecus and Paranthropus and so deserve their own genera. British evolutionary biologist, Richard Dawkins also believes there could be several species belonging to the genus of Paranthropus, but this is hotly debated.

All three species of Paranthropus share similar features, a small body and a strong or robust built skull. Including large lower jaw with extremely large molar teeth. The brain is relatively small and ranged from four hundred and twenty cubic centimeters for the Paranthropus aethiopicus to five hundred and twenty cubic centimeters for Paranthropus boisei and Paranthropus robustus. At this time Paranthropus robustus and boisei brain size was forty percent the size of modern humans and significantly larger brain cavity than the previous Australopithecus.

The skull features were ape-like, with a flat forehead and a prominent brow on the eye bridge or above the eyes. The face was rather broad with flaring cheekbones. Paranthropus aethropus had a more projecting face than the other two species of Paranthropus, which had shorter, flatter faces. The spinal cord passed through the centre of the skull base, indicating Paranthropus stood and walked upright. The males of the species had a massive bony ridge across the top of the skull, called a sagittal crest, which worked as an anchor for their powerful jaw muscles.

Compared to their back molar teeth, their front teeth or incisors and canines were very small. The molar teeth were very effective for crushing and grinding tough foods. Their jaws were large and robust and powerful as they were attached with large muscles to the sagittal crest.

Paranthropus boisei and robustus were slightly larger than Australopithecus africanus. Paranthropus aethiopicus however is harder to determine as skeletal evidence is missing, but appears to be much larger than the other two species. Males were significantly larger than females. As opposed to human rib cages, which are barrel shaped, Paranthropus ribcages seem to be cone shaped.

Paranthropus fossil evidence suggests their legs are human like, displaying the ability to walk upright, their arms are long compared to the legs, suggesting they could touch just above the knee when standing straight. The pelvis is similar to that of Australopithecus. Suggesting, it was ideal for walking, but not as efficiently as modern man.

It is suggested that these species lived in social groups with maybe one male and several females, similar to modern Gorillas. There is some debate if Paranthropus had controlled fire, as there is evidence they were making and using stone tools.

Paranthropus would have lived in open savannahs and woodlands, where they would
have dominated. There is also evidence the
environment of Africa was becoming drier at
this time one and a half million years ago.

Tooth wear suggests they would have eaten
mainly tough vegetation and hard foods such
as nuts, roots and seeds. They may also have
eaten some meat, but not very often.

Paranthropus aethiopicus

First discovered in 1985 by Biologist Anthropologist Alan Walker of Pennsylvania
State University in America in West Turkana, Kenya. West discovered a skull, which
is black in colouration because of its preser-
vation caused by high levels of Manganese.
The skull is dated as two and a half million
years. The skulls features are quite primitive
and share many similarities with Australopithecus afarensis, suggesting it is a direct
descendant.

This species is still very much a mystery to
paleoanthropologists, as very few remains
have been discovered.

Anthropologists are not all in agreement that
Paranthropus aethiopicus gave rise to Paranthropus boisei and Paranthropicus robustus
as the skull is very similar to that of Australopithecus afarensis, but the Paranthropus
aethiopicus jaw suggests it lived in savannahs and woodland. Which, is compatible

with previous finds and confirming that Australopithecus and Paranthropus are on the branch of evolution with the Homo genus.

An evident feature of the skull is the sagittal crest along the top of the skull. This would have served as an anchor for the powerful muscles supporting the lower jaw allowing this species a powerful motion when chewing.

Paranthropus boisei

In 1955, fossilised remains were discovered that has scientists baffled. In 1958, British archeologist and naturalist, Louis Leakey along with his wife Mary were excavating in the Olduvai Gorge in Tanzania. Leakey had convinced the scientific world, what defined the first human ancestor was the use of tools. He had spent the last twenty two years trying to find the maker of those tools and prove his theory correct. They had found plenty of tools. But, had not yet found the tool maker.

On the 17 July 1959, Louis Leakey was bed-ridden while recovering from Influenza. He had no idea this day was to become the high point of his career. While his wife, Mary was away from the camp walking their dogs she suddenly spotted a shape that was familiar among the rocky surface. She had found the top of a skull.

After coaxing Louis to the site she had found the skull and realising the skulls discovery was in the same geological layer the tools had been found in, so the logic was undeniable, this must be the tool maker, The skull also did not belong to any Homo species that had earlier thought to had been the first tool makers. Leakey named this specimen, Paranthropus boisei, named after his financial sponsor, Charles Boisei.

Leakey's find had a small brain but massive jaws and teeth. The jaws were anchored by massive muscles that were also anchored to the top of the skull, known as the Sagittal crest or ridge that runs along the top of the skull from the front of the skull to the back, that supports these powerful muscles that supports a strong chewing action.

Paranthropus boisei is believed to have descended from the earlier Paranthropus aethiopicus, who inhabited the same geographical area just a few hundred thousand years earlier. Paranthropus boisei did live alongside other species of early human during its one million year existence, which makes it one of many side branches of human evolution.

An earlier debate was cleared up in 1975, when a Paranthropus boisei specimen along with a Homo erectus specimen were discovered together in the same sedimentary layer, indicating they did co-exist together. Further discoveries have been made that confirms that both species lived in the same geographic area at the same time one million, seven hundred and fifty thousand years ago.

Louis Leakey examining fossilised skulls at Olduvai Gorge

Mary Leakey's discovery has been nick-named, Nutcracker man because of its obvi-ous diet of hard or rough foods such as nuts, seeds and ground tubers. The molars and premolars are very large, especially in width, with very thick enamel and the front teeth are very small, suggesting the Paranthropus boisei did the majority of its chewing to-wards the back of the mouth. The facial fea-tures are massive and positioned far forward, the nose is very large, The sagitttal crest is positioned more towards the front of the skull, suggesting the Paranthropus boisei's chewing muscles were positioned further front than previous Paranthropus aethiopicus.

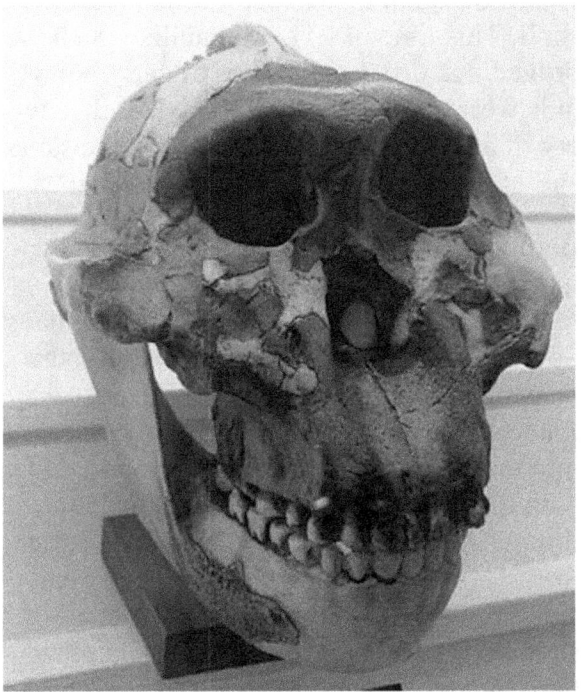

Reconstruction of Paranthropus boisei

The males were much larger than the females. Males weighed sixty eight kilograms and females weighed forty five kilograms, and lived in grassy savannahs and wetlands. Grassy areas close to water sources such as streams and lakes.

In 1960 Louis Leakey changed his mind about Parathropus boisei being the first tool maker in the human evolutionary time line, when Mary again made a startling discovery that turned the scientific world upside down when she again by accident, found another skull. This time of a Homo habilis which proved that different species of early hominids were co-existing in Africa. Her discovery of a Homo habilis was dated as the same age of the Paranthropus boisei specimen.

Before 1960 it was believed the human evolutionary model consisted of a single line from the earliest ancestor to modern humans. Somewhere in the middle there had to be a missing link between the two. When Leakey found Parathropus boisei, it was accepted into the single line in human evolution. Now with the discovery of Homo habilis, Paranthropus boisei had to be placed in a separate line, where boisei and habilis are existing, side by side, which made a whole paradigm shift from how science viewed human evolution. Suddenly, what was viewed as a single line of descent was now broken up into several lines to form a giant family tree.

Some species are evolutionary dead ends. They evolved, then became extinct. Others seem to be part of a line that leads ultimately to humans.

Paranthropus robustus

The first specimen of Paranthropus robustus was discovered by a school boy in 1938, in kromdraai, the boy Gert Terblanche showed the specimen to Scottish paleonthropologist Robert Broom of the Transvaal Museum in Johannesburg South Africa. The same year Broom visited the site of a sediment filled cave in Gauteng, southeast of Johannesburg. Broom called the specimen Paranthropus robustus.

Broom excavated the site over the next decade, discovering additional specimens now attributed to this species, with a dating of one million two hundred thousand years and two million three hundred years ago. He initially realised the Paranthropus species from the sagittal crest apparent on the head, as is with the previous Paranthropus species. At least one hundred and thirty fossilised specimens have been found contributing to the Paranthropus robustus.

Brain size of this species is a bit larger than the typical chimpanzee.

Paranthropus robustus definitely existed while stone tools were being made and used, though it remains unclear to what extent. The robustus brain was certainly bigger than previous generas.

The teeth are comparable to the previous Paranthropus boisei. Much larger than the previous Australopithecus suggesting the species also concentrated their chewing action at the back of the jaw. The jaw supported by massive muscles that were anchored at the top of the head by the Sagittal crest suggesting the diet consisted of hard gritty foods, such as nuts and tubers since they lived in open woodland and savannahs.

CHAPTER FIVE

Early Humans

The categorisation of early humans involved the evolution of the early homo genus about two million years ago in Africa. The Homo genus is of cause the genera where modern humans belong, the Homo sapiens. The most noticeable and important feature defining the genus homo from earlier species is the increase in brain or cranial capacity from twenty seven cubic inches or in scientific terms, 450cc, cc meaning cranial capacity in the earlier Australopithecus garhi to the first known homo species, the Homo habilis, who had a brain capacity of 37 cubic inches or 600cc (cranial capacity). The brain capacity from Homo habilis to homo ergaster to Homo erectus and homo heidelbergensis again had doubled. The homo genus has certainly experienced a major leap in evolution from previous species of pre-human lineages.

The advent of the Homo genus is widely regarded as the first evidence of where stone tools were in use. Although this is becoming more disputed now as evidence is surfacing that early stone tools were in use as long ago as three million years ago, as pointed out earlier in this book. The advent of the first homo species also coincides with the beginning of the Quaternary ice age. Which, is the beginning of the current ice age as the earth is technically still in this glaciation as is with the evident polar ice caps and various glaciers world wide.

The homo genus also involves the now extinct Neanderthals, which existed in south Europe around twenty four thousand years ago. Neanderthal is considered the last relative to modern humans in the evolutionary process, although a discovery in 2003 being the Homo floresiensis suggests the last relative to modern humans became extinct twelve thousand years ago.

The existence of the Homo genus is a story of mixture and migration. Eventually occupying every continents and area of the earth, leading up to the modern day. Throughout its history the homo genus have repeatedly migrated from Africa to occupy Europe and Asia, the Americas, Oceania, then eventually the rest of the world, beginning with homo erectus around one and a half million years ago. The areas in Africa formerly inhabited by earlier human species, being the savannahs are, now being inhabited by modern day chimpanzees.

The name homo originates from the latin word humanus meaning human being.

Not all recognised Homo species are direct descendants of all modern Homo sapiens, for example, Neanderthal and Denisova hominin but I will include them in this chapter, as they are essential for explaining the separation into other homo species leading up to the diversity of all humans occupying different regions of the planet today.

Although neanderthal are now extinct, their descendants certainly are not extinct. About seventy thousand years ago, some Homo sapiens, sapiens met and some bred with the Neanderthal. Some of the group left to populate Europe, Asia, Australia and later the Americas. A subgroup among them met and bred with the Denisovan. Some of this group migrated and populated Melanesia. Recent genomic evidence suggests at least thirty thousand years ago three major subspecies existed, those being the Denisovan, Neanderthal and the Cro-magnon. The cro-magnon were the first true human species.

Homo gautengensis

Earlier claimed to belong to the Australopithecus genus, then claimed to belong rather to the Homo ergaster and Homo habilis species. This species has had a rather unsettled history since its earlier discovery in 1977. A partial skull found in the Skerkfontein Caves in Gauteng near Johannesburg. Until biological anthropologist Darren Curnoe of the University of New South Wales in Australia in 2010 argued the species actually belong to the earliest Homo species and named the species Homo gautengensis.

Considered a possible close relative instead of a direct ancestor to modern humans. The Homo gautengensis had a relatively small brain and large teeth, indicating its diet consisted of mainly vegetation and plant material, though there is evidence this species may have used fire and could be the first known species to master fire as fossils also contain burnt animal bones.

The fossils discovered so far include a partial skull, several jawbones and teeth. These are dated at one million, eight hundred thousand years to one million, five hundred thousand years ago, making it the earliest known homo species though it may not have any direct ancestry to modern humans.

Homo habilis

Known simply as Handy Man, Homo habilis is known to be the first known direct ancestor to the modern human in the Homo genus. There is however still some debate whether Homo gautengensis holds that status. But, further discoveries and studies may put some light to such claims. First discovered and named in 1962 by Mary and Louis Leakey in Tanzania, east Africa, as mentioned in the previous chapter. Discoveries so far include a lower jaw and teeth. Studies conclude that Homo habilis had a brain size double that of Australopithecus sediba. and considerably smaller than modern humans. The teeth are smaller as opposed to the earlier Australopithecus species. A major discovery was in 1986 when anthropologists Donald Johanson and Tim White included the upper and lower legs indicating Homo habilis was short and had disproportionate arms, suggesting they were mainly living on the ground, stood and walked upright. But, still ventured among trees. Possibly for their diet of fruit, leaves and also to, avoid predators.

Reconstruction of a Homo habilis skull

Homo habilis remains have been discovered with a number of stone tools. Much more advanced and sophisticated that previous species which gave them the advantage in hunting large animal prey. Homo habilis is the first known hominid to use fire for heating and cooking.

A study in 2000 indicates that Homo habilis would have co-existed with the Paranthropus boisei and possibly with the Homo erectus as they both would have existed at the same time as Homo habilis. Destroying an earlier view that pre-homo erectus species existed one after the other, in a single line of evolution from the first pre human ancestor to modern humans.

Homo rudolfensis

First assigned to the Homo habilis species, the Homo rudolfensis was discovered by anthropologist Richard Leakey and his wife, Meave in 1972 at Lake Rudolf, which is now lake Turkana in Kenya. The specimen, a skull was incorrectly dated as being three million years old. Recent technology has been able to date the fossil at one million, nine hundred thousand years old. Which means that homo rudolfensis would have co-existed with Homo habilis.

Similar to the previous Australopithecus genus, the Homo rudolfensis had larger premolar and molar teeth, which is a feature for some scientists to believe that this species could in fact be a relative to Australopithecus rather than a member of the Homo genus. The skull is too pronounced to be a member of the Australopithecus genus and suggests it was either a member of the Homo habilis species or a third species that has not been realized yet. Future discoveries may lead to confirmation of the rudolfensis species.

Homo ergaster

Widely considered as the African Homo erectus, Homo ergaster is believed to be the last Homo species to remain in Africa and the first Homo species to migrate out of Africa and eventually settle throughout Europe and Asia. Homo ergaster is now widely accepted as the early ancestor to Homo erectus species such as Homo heidelbergensis, Neanderthal who settled throughout Europe and the Asian Homo erectus.

First discovered by paleoanthropologist John Robinson from South Africa, who made the discovery of a lower jaw in 1949. The most complete skeletal remains were discovered in 1984 at lake Turkana in Kenya by paleoanthropologist Kamoya Kimeu of the National Museum of Kenya. The skeletal remains gained the name Turkana Boy. The remains are dated at one million, six hundred thousand years old. The members of Homo ergaster who chose to stay in Africa, disappear from the fossil record around one million four hundred, thousand years ago after existing for five hundred, thousand years. It is not clear why this species disappeared, indicating they went extinct at around that time.

It is also widely believed that Homo ergaster were the first to harness or control fire. It is also widely argued how they first started creating fires, whether it were from natural sources such as lightening strikes or artificial methods, such as striking or rubbing sticks together. The debate remains contentious.

Another "First" with this species is the use of a linguistic communication. The brain capacity was advancing from earlier Homo genus species, which led to the use of more advanced stone tools leading up to Homo erectus.

CHAPTER SIX

Homo Erectus

A common misconception around the Homo erectus species is the notion this is a single species belonging to the Homo genus, though it is not in any way incorrect either, as Homo erectus is generally accepted as the first Homo species to migrate out of Africa. The Homo erectus sub-species make up the species

There are ten sub-species owning the name of Homo erectus. These are species that migrated out of Africa and evolved differently in different areas of the World. An example is Homo erectus georgicus, which was first discovered by Georgian scientist David Lordkipanidze in 1991. In Dmanisi, Georgia a skull and jaw were discovered that has been dated to one million, eight hundred thousand years old and has since been classified as belonging to the Homo erectus group.

Location of discovery of Homo erectus georgicus

Inspired by Darwin's theory of evolution, Dutch anatomist Eugene Duboi in 1891 discovered a skullcap and femur in east Java, which he believed was a species, he named Pithecanthropus erectus. Which, was later named as belonging to the Homo erectus group.

One million, eight hundred thousand years ago, the migration from Africa would have begun with Homo erectus species over the Levantine corridor and Horn of Africa to Europe and Asia, followed by the Homo antecessor eight hundred thousand years ago and Homo heidelbergensis around six hundred thousand years ago. A brach of the Homo heidelgergensis would have later evolved to become the famous Neanderthal of South Europe.

Further Homo species evolved out of Africa and migrated to areas such as near east, south Asia, Australia, America, Pacific Islands, Taiwan etc.

Known as Java Man, Homo erectus was discovered in 1891 by Eugene Duboi from the Netherlands. Duboi was hugely inspired by Charles Darwin's theory of evolution and travelled intensively in search of early human fossilised remains as Darwin's 1859 publication of "On The Origin Of Species" suggests that early life evolved from Europe, this theory was not corrected until the twentieth century. The fossilised remains of a Skullcap and femur are dated at one million years old.

During the 1880's, the theory of evolution was in its infancy. The concept of evolution was very basic at this time, as Victorian England science believed that evolution would have been over a short period of time. During Victorian times a notion for the missing link was popular. The belief was that the earliest ancestor to modern humans would have shared ape and human features and characteristics. For instance, an ape face, with a modern human body. We now know such an example is ludicrous and is impossible according to the laws of speciation or the differences between genes and species. Time and no concept was held for the age of earth and the actual length of time for species to change and diversify. Which takes thousands and millions of years.

In October 1889 on the island of Sumatra in the Dutch East Indies as the monsoon season was beginning, Eugene Duboi, a former student of medicine in Amsterdam believed the missing link could be found where ape and man live side-by-side. For Duboi, his dream turned into a nightmare as he was suffering from malaria and failed to find any evidence supporting his beliefs. Duboi had invested everything he had into his obsession of finding the missing link between ape and modern man. He also had no experience in jungle environments especially during a monsoon season. His mission failed. He had no idea where to look. In 1891 Duboi was on the Island of Java he had begun his search again. He had recovered from malaria. His luck began to change.

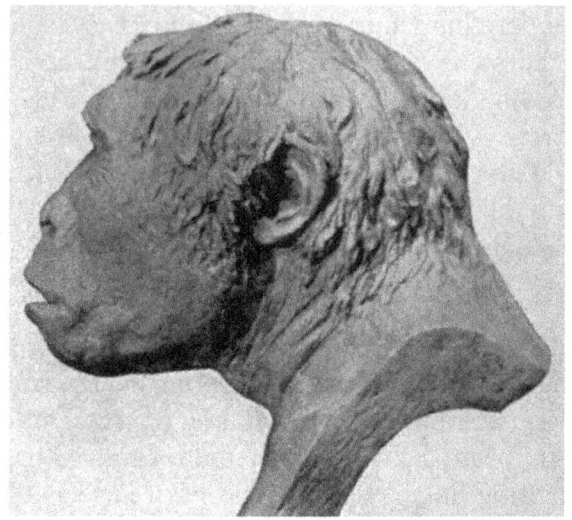

Reconstruction of Java Man, Homo erectus.

In Java, Duboi's team was bigger and was overseen by the Dutch Army. In October 1891, Duboi received another batch of skeletal remains from his team. Containing a fossilised skullcap. This sent Duboi into a frenzy of speculation as he could only compare the skullcap to the Neanderthal discovery forty years earlier, which had been dated as forty thousand years old. Duboi had no knowledge of any earlier ancient human ancestor.

The forests of Sumatra and Java held a large variety of ape species. Duboi knew this skull did not belong to any known ape species. It was finer and the brain cavity was very large in comparison to any known ape species. Duboi began to wonder if it was actually an earlier human ancestor, closer to our earlier ape like origins than Neanderthal. At this time, Duboi had no idea this skull cap was half a million to one million years old, considerably older than the previously discovered Neanderthal of forty thousand years. He considered if this specimen was indeed the missing link, Duboi realised the key was in the size of the brain. He had a formula to determine the brain size of a missing link. This formula was exactly half the size of a modern human and twice the size of an ape. When he measured the brain cavity of this specimen, he discovered is was the wrong size for his formula, The brain cavity was too big for a half way point, so was too big to be the ape like creature he had imagined. Another discovery of a complete leg bone, suggested this ancestor stood upright on two legs, like a human. He realised he could never change his evidence and declared to the Dutch government he had found the missing link between apes and humans. He named this species, Pithecanthus erectus, which is today called, Homo erectus, which originated in Africa eight hundred thousand years ago. Homo erectus gained the name *Java man*.

Another find in the Great Rift Valley in Kenya confirms this species originated in Africa. Confirming that modern man originated from common ancestors we share with great apes

Standing at about six feet tall, their bodies were the same shape as the modern human. Their brain size was two, thirds the size of ours, which allowed them to colonise Africa, Europe and Asia. Homo erectus was on the verge of becoming human. The main reason for this was for the first time in our evolution. Homo erectus had access to a high protein diet that included meat. There exists no evidence that Homo erectus was a hunter, but may have scavenged the meat from other predators, using their stone tools and weapons as a method to scare away these predators from a freshly killed prey.

The body was undergoing major changes. The body had developed sweat glands, which prevented the need to pant from the suns heat. Body hair was disappearing and voices were developing, paving the way for human speech.

Throughout evolution, every species of early human and animal were afraid of fire and ran away from it. Homo erectus was at a cross roads of evolution and mastered fire and used it for heating, lighting and cooking and maybe also had a method for scaring away predators, as Homo erectus were extremely vulnerable to these predators, especially at night time as they shared the same rocky shelters as most predatory animals. The use of fire would also play the part of an ancient security device against such danger.

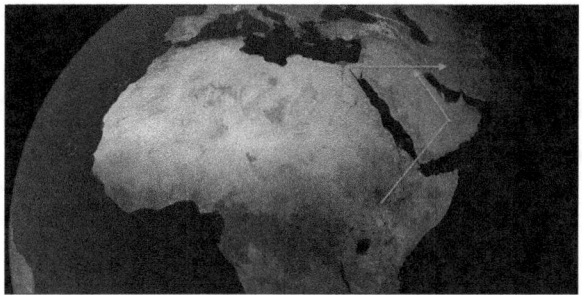

Early diversification and migration route through The Levantine corridor and Horn of Africa

Homo erectus georgicus

Although first suggested as a separate species, Homo erectus georgicus was discovered in Dmanisi in Georgia, present day Russia, this species is now described as a member of the Homo erectus group.

Aged at one million, eight hundred thousand years, the first fossils of a skull and jaw bone of an individual was discovered by Georgian Scientist David Lordkipanidz in 1991. Stone tools were also discovered in the sediment along with various animal bones. Initially, scientists believed they had recovered remains of a Asian Homo species, but further studies suggested they belonged to a separate species, so renamed it Homo erectus georgicus.

The skull is small and primitive to the modern human skull and the most primitive found outside Africa and suggests that males were significantly larger than females, which is today less evident in modern humans living in Europe. Homo erectus georgicus was the first Homo species to exist in Europe.

Homo erectus tautavelensis

Existing in France around four hundred and fifty thousand years ago. Homo erectus tautavelensis was first discovered in the Arago cave in Tautavel in France in 1964 by geologist Marcel de Serres from the University of Montpellier in southern France.

The fossilised evidence consists of a skull and a lower jaw from a male and a female between the age of twenty years to no older than forty years of age. Brain size is suggested to be similar to that of Homo erectus georgicus. The shape is similar to that of Homo sapiens.

No ash or evidence of fire were present in the cave, suggesting the Homo erectus tautavelensis may not have controlled or used fire.

Homo erectus soloensis

Now classified as a member of the Homo erectus group, Homo erectus soloensis was initially believed the be a Homo sapien as its culture seemed advanced for an earlier species in the Homo genus.

Generally known as Solo Man. Homo erectus soloensis was initially believed to be an ancestor to the Australian Aboriginal. Further studies have concluded that this was not the case. Fossil dating in 2011 suggests a date of five hundred and fifty thousand years old to one hundred and forty three thousand years old.

Specimens belonging to Homo erectus soloensis were discovered along the Bengawan Solo River in Java of a skull and teeth and two leg bone fragments, displaying features that are gracile and more anatomical features, along with many stone tools.

Homo erectus pekinensis

First discovered in 1927 in Peking, China, which is now Beijing and named as *Peking man*. A number of partial skulls, jaws, teeth and some skeletal bones were discovered along with many stone tools in caves near present day, Beijing in Zhaoudoudian. Dated to be around three hundred thousand and five hundred thousand years old.

Until his death in 1934, Canadian paleoanthropologist Davidson Black initially made the discovery. But, German anatomist Franz Weidenreich went on and studied the specimens until leaving China in 1941. Some casts were shipped to America for protection during World War II. Unfortunately the original specimens disappeared during the war and have never been recovered.

Anatomist Franz Weidenreich concluded that Homo erectus pekinensis is a direct ancestor to modern man, in particular the modern Chinese. Chinese geneticist Jin Li in 1999 confirmed that modern Chinese ancestors originated from Africa, like all modern humans.

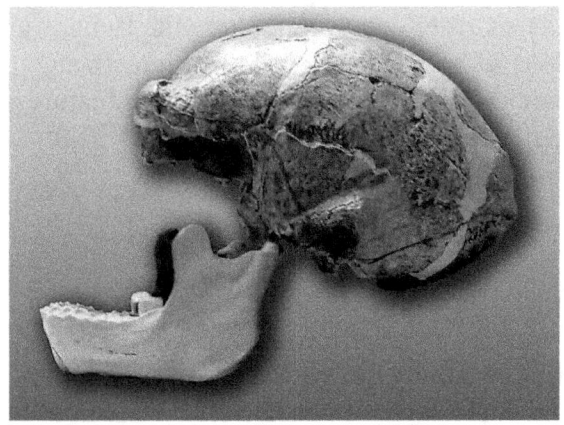

Cast reconstruction of "Peking Man" Skull, missing facial skeletal bones

Homo cepranensis

Available knowledge to this species is based on a single Skullcap discovered in 1994, in the province of Frosinone, southeast of Rome in Italy by archeologist Italo Biddittu. This species has been named as Ceprano Man.

The fossilised remains of Homo cepranensis is dated at three hundred and fifty thousand years to five hundred thousand years old and seem to represent ancestors of later species that dominated Europe and an early ancestor to Neanderthal.

There is not yet enough evidence to completely analyse this individual.

Homo antecessor

Dated at one million years to eight hundred, thousand years ago, Homo antecessor has been determined to be one of the earliest ancestor of human species existing in Europe six hundred thousand years to two hundred and fifty thousand years ago.

First discovered by Spanish paleoanthropologist Eudald Carbonell and Biological scientist Juan Luis Arsuaga in 1997 of a Maxilla or an irregular shaped bone that shapes the upper jaw that was later determined to belong to a ten year old male. A further eighty specimens belonging to ten individuals of the Homo antecessor were later discovered in Atapuerca in Spain. These fossilised remains show signs of the skin being cut and removed. Indicating Homo antecessor may have practiced cannibalism.

Studies suggest the brain size of Homo antecessor is slightly smaller than the brain size of modern man, the Teeth indicate that this species had the same development stages as the modern Homo sapiens. The height between individual male and female would have been comparable to the modern human height.

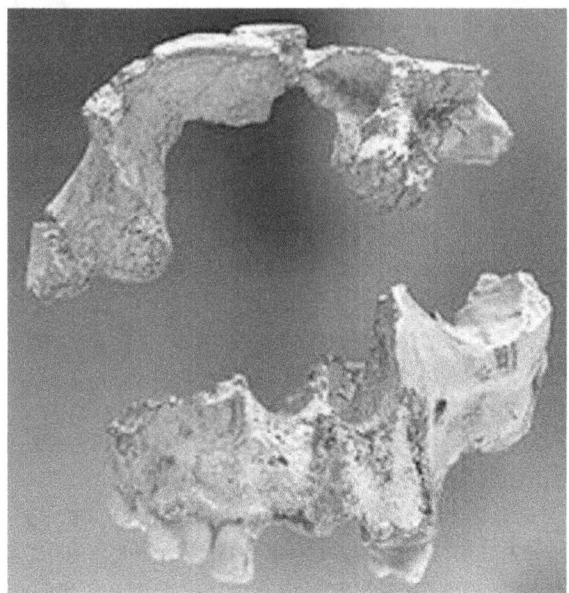

Fossilised remains of Homo antecessor

In 2010 Stone tools extraordinarily similar to those found with Homo antecessor remains were also found in Norfolk, England, suggesting this species may have also existed as far north as the UK as early as nine hundred and fifty thousand years ago.

Homo heidelbergensis

A direct ancestor to both Neanderthal and European Homo sapiens, Homo heidelbergensis is named after the Heidelberg University in Ohio, USA. Homo heidelbergensis had a slightly larger brain capacity of modern humans. The body was also slightly more muscular than modern humans, standing at an average of six foot tall. Indicating most populations of heidelbergensis were "giants" as compared to earlier and later species. Their stone tool technology was also very advanced compared to earlier implements.

The species was first discovered in 1907, after a workman, Daniel Hartmann spotted a jaw. Hartmann handed the specimen to professor Otto Schoetensack from the University of Heidelberg who studied the remains and named it Homo heidelbergenisis. The fossil had been dated at four hundred thousand to six hundred thousand years old.

Available evidence suggests they possessed the ability for audible sound, or able to communicate in a rudimentary way and able to differentiate between various sounds. Homo heidelbergensis were evidently hunter

as primitive spears were discovered in Schoningen in northern Germany believed to belong to the heidelbergensis as dating of these projectiles are similar to that of Homo heidelbergensis. Suggesting different sustenance diets and methods of hunting from earlier homo species, Very similar to the New Zealand Maori who preferred to use clubs instead of spears.

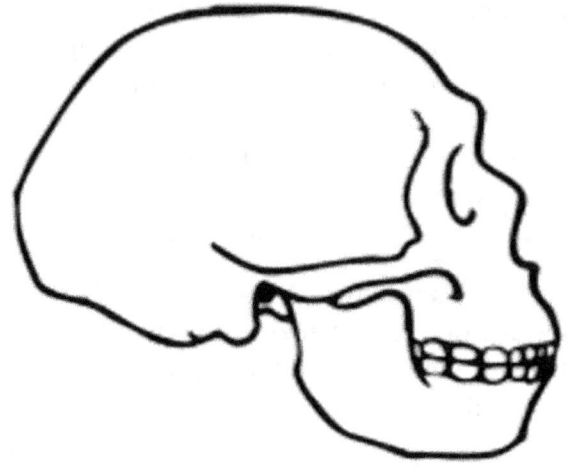

Impression of Homo heidelbergensis skull

In 1994, further fossilised remains have been found in Britain, along with hand axes dating back four hundred and seventy eight thousand years, indicating heidelbergensis existed in both Great Britain and France. Fossil discoveries are also indicating, Spain was also inhabited three hundred and fifty thousand years ago by Homo heidelgergensis.

Homo neanderthalensis

Closely related to modern humans, the Neanderthal were closer to today's humans than their African ancestors.

In 1856 in the Neander valley near Dusseldorf in Germany as workers who were paid a few pence a day, were digging for Limestone for the local chemical industry in a cave. As the surface layer was being removed and thrown away a spade hit an object that did not have the same sound as a rock. When removed, they discovered the object had the shape of a human skullcap. The workers feared this may be the remains of a murder victim or a Bear and showed it to their supervisor. The supervisor thought it was very interesting and thought nothing of it, then ordered the skull be thrown away with the rest of the rubble excavated from the cave this skull was found in. A few moments later, the supervisor remembered a local school teacher who may be interested in the skull fragment. What the supervisor did not realise was the skull fragment was seeing the light of day for the first time in over forty thousand years. The school teacher, amateur naturalist and former anatomy student Johann Fuhlrott.

The moment Fuhlrott saw the skull, he realised it was something extraordinary. He realised it was fossilised and certainly was not an animal and it certainly was not the skullcap of a modern human being. An upper leg bone or femur, were also presented to Fuhlrott. He believed the remains might be that of an early ancestor to modern man. The remains were eventually presented to anatomist Hermann Schaaffhausen in 1857. The partial skeletal remains indicate the Neanderthal brain was similar in size to the Homo sapien genus perhaps slightly larger. Their arms and legs were stronger than modern man.

Reconstruction of Neanderthal

The environment at this time in Europe, forty thousand years ago, was fluctuating as the northern glaciation was advancing further south. Three hundred years later, the area which the Neanderthal were discovered in the Neander valley was under a half mile of ice and glaciers. To survive in such extreme conditions, a diet of nutrient rich and high protein meat would have supported Neanderthal communities of up to a dozen individuals. They were very strong with a large brain as compared to earlier species of early human. Their stone tools were sophisticated and were the method or tools for their survival and needed to be well maintained as the numbers of prey were diminishing as the glaciers advanced. Their spears failing during a hunt would have been devastating for their family or community.

This may have been a discovery which led to Charles Darwin to believe that Humans evolved from Europe, as Neanderthalensis was first discovered in 1856, Three years before Darwins Book "On the origin of species" was published and could have influenced his beliefs for his later book "The descent of man" which was published in 1871, the book where Darwin made the claim.

The early Neanderthals would have appeared in Europe as long ago as six hundred thousand years ago. The genetic makeup of modern humans indicate that the Neanderthal would have mixed and interbred with Homo heidelbergensis at some stage, as modern Eorpeans and Asians are one to four percent Neanderthal, being the main considering factor when neanderthalensis were classified as belonging to the Homo genus. Neanderthalensis are related to Australopithecus and Homo habilis along with Homo ergaster.

No fossil evidence of Neanderthal existing in Africa, suggesting they would have evolved from the earlier Homo erectus and dispersed into most areas of Europe. At their peak, it is estimated there would have been a population of at least seventy thousand in areas such as Western Europe and south coastal areas in Britain, central Europe and the Balkans, Ukraine, Gibraltar, and the Levant. The geological conditions such as a glaciation would have prevented the migration north of the fiftieth parallel.

Evidence suggests that Neanderthal were largely carnivores and effectively hunted. Recent evidence in 2010 from a researcher from the US reported finding cooked vegetable in the teeth of a Neanderthal, which was in stark contrast to an earlier belief that Neanderthal was exclusively carnivore. They made and used what can be considered, advanced tools than previous species and communicated in some form of language. An excavation site in the Ukraine suggests they also built their shelters from animal bones such as mammoth tusks and leg bones. Though the last known habitat for Neanderthal was in a cave on the south coast of Gibraltar suggests they were also cave dwellers.

Denisovan

A close relative to the Neaderthal was first discovered in Russia's Siberian Altai Mountains in 2008. A report published in 2011 claims that one percent of their genes are present in modern Asian populations and six percent in modern day Australian Aborigines and Melanesians.

The remains discovered in the Denisova caves were bone fragments of a fifth finger of a juvenile woman. A toe bone and a tooth have since been discovered in north China and south Asia from which genetic material has been gathered. The artifacts also include a bone bracelet, which were dated at forty thousand years old. Genetic testing shows the remains excavated in Siberia are from a Neanderthal and Denisovan offspring.

Very little is known so far about the Denisovan as the remains discovered are inadequate to give any indication of anatomical features.

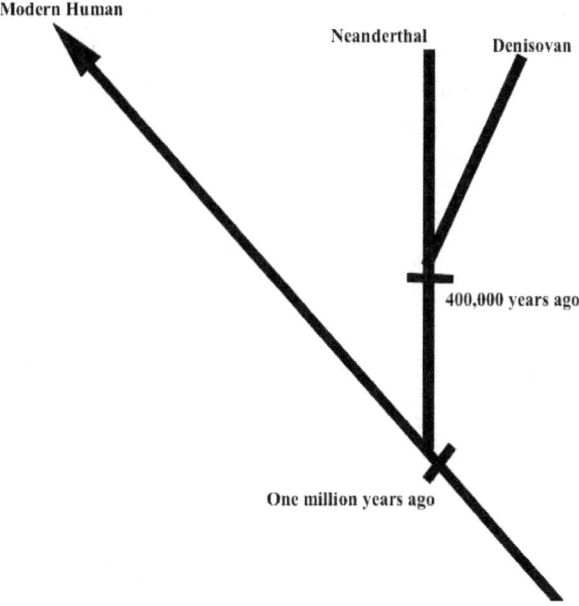

Evolutionary timeline from Homo sapiens to Neanderthal and Denisovan

Testing shows that the Homo sapiens, Neanderthal and Denisovans originated from a common ancestor, one million years ago. Neanderthal and Denisovan ancestor split into their own lineages four hundred thousand years ago. The Neanderthal lineage migrated northwestward into west Asia and Europe. The Denisovan lineage migrated into East Asia.

Modern Humans ancestors stayed in Africa until sixty five thousand years ago, until migrating into Europe and Asia, where they encountered and mixed with the Neanderthal and Denisovan groups. Genetic testing also revealed the Neanderthal and Denisovan also bred and their descendents are still alive today throughout Asia.

CHAPTER SEVEN

Anatomically Modern Humans

The term anatomically modern humans is an anthropological term, referring to the early Homo sapiens displaying a range of features consistant with modern Homo sapiens. Direct descendent from Homo heidelbergensis and its closest relative Homo neanderthalensis and leading up to today's modern Homo sapiens.

Anatomically modern humans are distinguished from earlier human species with their significantly smaller brow ridge just above the eyes. In today's Homo sapiens, that brow ridge is practically none existent as compared to earlier species. Modern humans have a flatter more vertical forehead as compared to earlier human ancestors who had a more backward sloping forehead. Their skeletons are more gracile from the earlier robust skeletons. The chin is also more prominent as compared to Homo sapien ancestors.

Two hundred thousand years ago, the North and South regions of earth were in the grips of a dramatic climate change, causing unstable environments. Africa was not immune to this dramatic change, which led to the migration out of Africa for Homo sapiens earlier ancestors. They hunted and gathered and evolved behaviours and habits that dramatically assisted their adaptations to cope with these environmental changes.

Mitochondrial Eve

To begin with, I would like to point out a misconception held by creationists that the existence of mitochondrial Eve is proof that Scientists have admitted to their claim that all humans originated from the Biblical claim of Adam and Eve. This is a fallacy, as science relies of evidence, which can be tested and proved, not mythology or cultural beliefs.

Although the mitochondrial Eve is scientific proof that all existing humans did evolve from one female, does not assume that a chromosomal Adam existed at the same time as the mitochondrial Eve. It also does not assume that the mitochondria Eve was the only female existing at that time. In fact, there were tens of thousands of other females existing at that time. The chromosomal Adam actually existed fifty thousand to eighty thousand years after the mitochondrial Eve. The mitochondrial Eve was the originator to the human X chromosome and Adam is responsible for the Y chromosome in modern humans.

Mitochondria Eve is the most recent maternal linear ancestor, not the most recent common ancestor

Chromosomal Adam is the most recent paternal linear ancestor, not the most recent common ancestor

The genetic material, known as the DNA in a cells nucleus controls the cell. It brings in nutrients from various parts of the body. Then makes hormones, proteins and other chemicals. The cytoplasmic matrix, or the cytoplasm contains tiny organelles that are commonly referred to as Mitochondria, which are past down from generation to generation by the mother, which are commonly referred to as "energy factories" of the cell.

The field of human genetics, refer to mitochondrial Eve as the most common maternal ancestor, or the matrilineal ancestor of modern humans. Or, all living humans evolved from mitochondrial Eve on their mothers side, as the Mitochondrial DNA every human possesses is descended from their mothers, including the Y chromosome by definition, although the chromosomal Adam and mitochondrial Eve lived thousands of years apart.

Ancestors to modern humans were evolving into their own distinct species two hundred thousand years ago. This is the exact time that mitochondrial Eve existed. Mitochondrial eve most likely lived in east Africa, as the first Homo sapiens were becoming distinct from their earlier ancestor and other human sub-species.

Mitochondrial Eve existed earlier than the ancestor of Homo heidelbergensis and before the emergence of Homo neanderthalensis and before the migration out of Africa.

It is relatively easy to trace the lineage back to mitochondrial Eve. The mitochondrial DNA is traced unmixed from mother to children of both sexes back through the generations through the maternal side, until the DNA lineage converges. Mitochondrial

DNA accumulates mutations every three thousand five hundred years on average. DNA mutations are the driving force for the evolutionary process. A certain number of variations will survive and pass onto modern lineages as a distinct lineage.

Chromosomal Adam

Chromosomal Adam gets its name from the Biblical Adam, and does however cause misconceptions. Chromosomal Adam was not and did not need to be the first male. He in fact lived with thousands of other males, including his father, but no other males at his time produced an unbroken male line leading to modern humans. Only his descendents survived. Chromosomal Adam is responsible for the Y chromosome all males possess in their mitochondria to this day.

Chromosomal Adam lived around one hundred and forty two thousand years ago. Contrary to creationists wish, Chromosomal Adam and Mitochondrial Eve would not have met during their life times.

The right place at the right time?

The first primates evolved eight million years ago. Modern humans emerged from Africa and began their independent evolutionary journey two hundred, thousand years ago, in doing so, conquering the world by twenty thousand years ago and witnessing the end of our closest relative, The Neanderthal who had established themselves quite successfully throughout western Europe, but later became extinct. Why was this? Was it a simple case of "being in the right place at the right time?" Throughout modern Homo species advancements and diversifications, many Human like species have evolved and established, just to die out in the past.

Neanderthal died out around thirty thousand years ago, during the Earths last glacial period or ice age. Modern humans at this time preferred the warmer tropical and sub tropical climates where they could exist relatively comfortably and spread out, where as the Neanderthal remained in northern regions. As the glacial conditions advanced from the north, Neanderthals would have been faced with a decreasing supply of resources. Our direct ancestors did interbreed with Neanderthal. We know this, because today's Human's are between one and four percent Neanderthal.

Some scientists suggest Neanderthal perished because of this interbreeding. Suggesting, eventually the Human genomes, which were more dominant over the Neanderthal genomes eventually guaranteed the Neanderthal extinction. Or, the species bred out of existence.

The Homo genus is very adaptable, meaning they can adapt and exist in many environments, which is why we had so much success after leaving Africa and moving into so many areas from the arctic circle to the Antarctic, until the Neanderthal faced their demise.

When faced with an Ice age, it is always best to be in the right place.

Since migrating and evolving out of Africa, the ancestors to Homo sapiens have slowly, but surely conquered the world. Within one hundred and twenty five thousand years ago, they had reached the near East. Populations had reached south Asia within fifty thousand years ago. Populations had reached throughout Europe where they continued to replace the Neanderthal by forty three thousand years ago. Towards the Southern hemisphere they had reached Australia by forty thousand years ago, east Asia by thirty thousand years ago.

The earliest Homo sapien advance into the Americas is very much a source of contention to this day. The migration into North America is believed to be around thirty thousand years ago to fourteen thousand years ago. The migrations into the pacific Islands began three thousand years ago and ended with New Zealand's earliest populations around two thousand years ago.

CHAPTER EIGHT

MODERN HUMANS

As a human being, everything about you such as the shape of your face, the ability to walk on both legs and the way you see the world is what makes you the person you are This can be traced back to ancient Africa over eight million years ago in the fossilised remains of our ancient ancestor laying deep underground and throughout our history in our bones, flesh and genes. Teaching us how our ancestors struggled for their survival and evolved into the people we are. We left behind the other apes and became the only one of our species to survive through learning from each other and adjusting to the many different and changing environments that faced our ancestors. The world has changed over the last eight million years and so did our ancestors, in ways that may be hard for us to comprehend in the modern world.

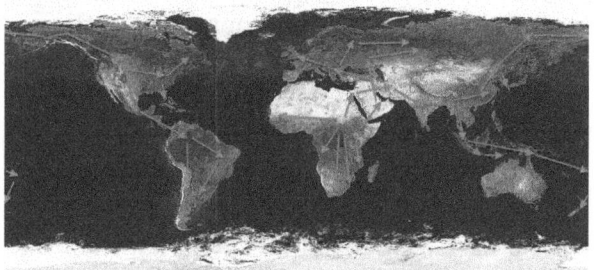

Over the last One million, eight hundred thousand years, Humans now occupy every area of the planet.

Since deciding to stand upright and walk on both legs, our early ancestors body has changed and diversified over the past six million years. When observing the modern gorilla their feet have more mobility, adapted for climbing trees as opposed to walking, as opposed to humans who walk primarily upright their big toes are more outright pointing than the earlier humans, giving easier ability for climbing. The human toes are all more forward facing and inline with each other.

Early hominid skulls have changed and grown as the brain has grown, earlier ancestor have larger brow ridges above their eyes, where as homo sapiens have a slight brow ridge that is barely visible and a more upright forehead as compared to earlier backward slanting foreheads as indicative with the Neanderthal forehead. The body skeletal bones have dramatically changed to allow a more adept stance and movement of humans. The pelvis is more centralised to give rotating movement for running and walking. The spinal column is in the shape of a lazy or slight "S" shape than other animals living on earth. The spinal column increasingly becomes larger and thicker towards the base of the spine to support the upper body structure. The Bum or the Gluteus Maximus are large muscles that contract and stretch during leg movement to give more power and energy for running long distances.

Another outstanding development throughout our evolutionary journey into modern humans was the changes and growth of our brains. From the earliest ancestors, the brain size has steadily increased from the earliest common ancestor with the modern apes, to double its size in the Australopithecus. Then the brain size doubled again with the Homo heidelbergensis and the European Neanderthal. In the modern human, the brain size is four times the volume of our earliest ancestor.

Its hard to figure out just why the brain grew so much by just looking at the fossilised remains of our earliest ancestor, but by taking a look at the environment they lived in, many different reasons can be looked at.

The crucible of early evolution or, the Rift Valley in eastern Africa, can give many clues of the driving force of our early evolution by looking at the rocks to give some insight into the environment, many millions of years ago. Studies of rocks in the Rift Valley indicate the environment was rapidly changing over a very short time of just a few hundred years, in the blink of an eye in evolutionary terms. Our ancestors would have had an extremely hard life and would have had to adapt to the changing environment very quickly, or face extinction. This rate of change would have made adapting very difficult. Our earliest ancestors did adapt by changing their behaviour, only the cleverest found ways to find food and water that allowed them to survive, change and pass on their genes. It is believed the larger brain allowed our ancestor to adapt and flourish in a large diversity of different environments.

One particular driving force for the evolution of the human brain was the ability to make and use stone tools. This was a complicated method. Some areas of the Rift Valley are littered with remains of stone tool making debris. Indicating this was a learned practice, passed down by many generations as the rock first had to be quarried, then each individual rock had to be struck at a certain angle to get the best slither in order to shape the tool. These debris fields show the many attempts to create the right tool. Showing how fussy and particular these early humans were, and the lessons taught and learned by many in the art of creating these stone tools. The practice of making and using these tools would undoubtedly have found its benefits for the entire populations to learn and teach abilities from one another.

Making these stone tools would have had irreversible advantages to our early ancestors. For example, they would have had to have an idea or an abstract idea in their mind of what that finished tool will look like and how it will be used. This technique may well be responsible to other advancements throughout our evolution, such as the ability to communicate or, language. It is unknown when language first evolved. It is however believed this may have been around two hundred thousand years ago. Fossilised evidence cannot prove this as the vocal chords and vocal tracts exist as soft tissue and will not fossilise along with bones.

The brain size between the modern human and neanderthal are the same size, eliminating an earlier notion that the neanderthal were less intelligent that modern man, which leads scientists of today to believe the neanderthal were just as smart as modern humans, but did things differently.

Recent discoveries of remains found in modern day Gibraltar are indicating that the neanderthal stone tools were more advanced and specialised than previous human like ancestors and more specilised than the equivalent Homo heidelbergensis. Suggesting that Homo heidelbergensis may have learned to hone their tool making techniques from the neanderthal.

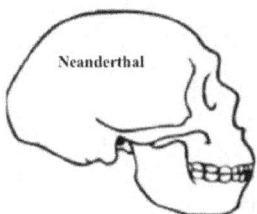 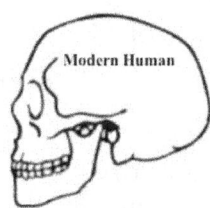

The Skull comparisons between Neanderthal and Modern Humans clearly display the feature differences between facial and brain size.

If neanderthal were more advanced and smarter than earlier humans, why did their population decline and Homo sapiens populations increase and thrive? As I mentioned, neanderthal were more intelligent than Homo heidelbergensis, but they lived differently than Homo heidelbergensis and also bred together, so its not really true to say that neanderthals are extinct as most modern humans carry neanderthal genes and will do for coming millennia. Humans were able to adapt to different environments easier than neanderthal and so thrived and spread out around the globe with more ease. For the neanderthal, an extended draught or extra cold winter would have been enough for a population decrease, where as humans were better able to adapt and thrive in different environments.

A major difference with an increasing brain size is the ability to learn from other individuals, this certainly would have been the case with early humans and neanderthal and many other earlier ancestor and cousins who co-habited together. This ability begins in humans from a very young age.

Children learn very quickly how to read minds of their peers and adults by learn how to manipulate and learn by reading facial expressions, such as an expression of happiness, anger, sorrow and movement, along with communication techniques.

A problem that evolution presented to humans was the small hips, required for walking upright. This presented a problem with childbirth. Compared to other mammals, human babies brain size is large, so causes sometimes fatal difficulties for women when giving birth. The opening of the birth canal is small which makes child birth difficult. Evolution has however provided a solution to this problem as a new born babies skull is soft and flexible, allowing for an easier birth.

The child's skull does not fuse or harden until after its birth, within its first year of life.

Comparative to other mammals, the human baby is born without the ability to control their bodies and the ability to make sense of their surroundings, their brains are immature, totally helpless and reliant on their parents. Its brain will continue to grow until the age of eight, but won't be until the child's mid teens until its brain is mature enough to cope with the outside world.

Until quite recently on the evolutionary time period, humans lived in small bands or groups as hunter-gatherers, dependent on the close proximity of water and wild life for hunting, until the time that agriculture and farming appeared with the domestication of cattle.

Six thousand years ago in the Indus valley and Egypt's Nile valley or Mesopotamia the first civilizations began to appear. Humans were beginning to form larger communities, towns and cities, merging or mixing many different groups of people. Governments were first formed along with military capabilities for protection, as a result some societies started trading and competing for resources with some wars between groups for domination.

Between three thousand and two thousand years ago, other civilizations and empires began to appear such as China, Persia, India, Rome and Greece, mainly through conflicts. Greece set down the foundation for Western culture. The first religion was formed at this time, Judaism and Hindu rising to prominence.

The collapse of the Roman Empire, which ended in 476, saw the beginning of the European middle ages, which gave rise to revolutionary ideas and technologies. An advance in urbanization in China gave rise to innovations such as science. Innovations also such as mathematics, metallurgy and philosophy were pioneered in India. The middle ages were also the golden age of Islam, with scientific and medical advancements in Muslim nations. Most practices in medicine from the golden age of Islam are still practiced today including the introductions into society of Hospitals, numerous medical procedures and trigonometry.

Throughout Europe the printing press came into existence, which led to the Renaissance. Over five hundred years, exploration and colonization resulted in much of the world coming under European sovereignty or control.

The seventeenth century bought the scientific revolution and the Industrial revolution in the nineteenth and twentieth centuries bringing major innovations such as rail and automobile travel and energy development.

Political ideologies such as representative democracy and communism were also developed during the industrial revolution.

Human Intelligence

Throughout this book you read about the evolution of modern humans from now extinct pre-human genera and species belonging to those genera. The evolutionary process leading from the earliest human ancestor up to the modern day humans. One aspect of the evolutionary process is the intelligence of those ancestors of prehuman ancestors and the increasing intelligence level.

What is Intelligence? There are various theories that try to answer this. There seems to be just as many theories as there are stars in the Universe. None seem to give any accurate explanation for a definition of Intelligence. Albert Einstein was told by one of his teachers that he was below average intelligence, yet he is the probably the most well known and most brilliant scientist ever to have lived. So, why was such a man judged to be below average intelligence? Why was it then that German News magazine Der Spiegel to declare Albert Einstein "Genius of the Century" and Time Magazine to declare him "Person of the Century" towards the end of the twentieth Century?

Intelligence is not based on an individuals education alone. Different aspects pertaining to intelligence includes" learned abilities, Common sense to apply that learned abilities and the natural abilities to include all three aspects into a certain arena, known as Intelligence.

An individuals "Brilliance" is the ability to apply all those aspects together into intelligent thought and practice. An example would be a Medical Doctor who may be accused of medical malpractice. Chances are high that the Doctor may have applied his learned ability to his decision or practice but failed to apply any common sense into his initial decision, therefore failed to naturally foresee or recognise any potential reaction or problem that could arise from such a decision. The malpractice could be a result of a certain misunderstanding of his learned ability, leading to the failed natural ability, which is to a degree, based on his common sense.

It has been said that any task or duty an individual carries out is ninety eight percent common sense. The other two percent is based on the individuals learned ability and their natural ability. Common sense and natural ability is inclusive of each other. A doctor or scientist who is considered Brilliant in their career is able to combine all three of the components that, when included make up an individuals Intelligence.

Since this book is based around scientific evidence and theory, another example could be the difference between science and pseudo science. Science is a latin word, meaning "Knowledge" and the word Pseudo, is also a latin word, meaning "false". A pseudo scientist may be educated around any aspect of science, but fails to apply any of the other two aspects I previously mentioned into his educated thought. This failure could be based on previous education that is corrupting his scientific education or personal beliefs that is reinforcing his or her predetermined ideals, thus basing their findings on their predetermined beliefs. Because of a lack of understanding of some of their understanding of their learned field.

The evolution of human intelligence would have begun around ten million years ago, as the Earth entered a warmer drier period, which ultimately led to drier conditions in northern Africa around 2.6 million years ago, resulting in the retreat of heavily forested regions into grassy savannah's then the formation of the Sahara desert. This change forced the early human ancestors to leave their previous habitat and favour the savannahs instead. This change of habitat would have made them vulnerable to predators such as big cats, which the heavier forests would have given them some protection from. This was the time the early human ancestors first started to rise on two feet and the first steps of mobility as bipedalism, or the ability to walk on both feet. Freeing their arms and hands for food gathering and later, the ability to make and use primitive tools and harness fire for warmth, cooking as well as the ability to pick up objects.

The concept we now accept as human intelligence would have begun at this time as hominids adapted to their new environments and became smarter and able to avoid large predators while living in open grassy savannahs. Rising up onto two feet would have given an ability to see further afield to spot any potential dangers, leading to a more efficient form of locomotion.

About five million years ago, the human brain began its rapid growth that will continue throughout the human evolutionary process. In doing so, increasing the intelligence level of pre-human species. One main factor for an increase in the intelligence would have been when humans started living in groups, as a learned ability, a new method or idea would have been discovered, then through experience would have been taught to others in that group or community, then defined as a new ability was honed through experience of a newer generation, then the more advanced method would have been taught to the next generation.

Abstract thought would have been crucial for the improvements of tools and art throughout the evolutionary history of humans. An idea and an imagination of what the implement would look like and its use would have been defined during the making process and techniques would have improved with every new generation.

The evolution of human intelligence is believed to have taken a great leap forward around seventy thousand years ago, at the time a volcano in Sumatra, known as Mount Toba, erupted, spreading volcanic ash worldwide for several years. The explosive eruption decreased the human population to about ten thousand in Africa. Being unprepared for the dramatic climate cooling as a result, those who managed to survive were those who were able to find new ways of keeping warm, finding new ways of finding food, which probably included the first tools and the ability to catch fish and later, ocean fishing as inland lakes and rivers froze as a result of the ice age of this time in earths history.

Throughout Human evolution, humans have had the mental ability to learn from experience, understand and implement abstract thought, adapt to different situations and also to use their knowledge to manipulate their environments.

As human communities grew, the intelligence also grew as well as other human traits such as altruism, as different relationships within the communities were formed and the ability to understand different emotions such as sadness and happiness and thoughts of others. Our closest relatives, the chimpanzee usually have social groups of around fifty. Humans commonly have social groups of around one hundred and fifty.

Society and Culture

Society and culture are different. But, they are inextricably linked, as culture is a product of an individuals mind. As a society consists of many individuals, that culture is a product of every individuals mind, belonging to that society. Every individual in a society relate to their shared common culture and traditions, that are learned from other members of a society. Cultures evolve as societies change. Different cultures can be moved into other cultures as a "sub culture" among a larger culture as people migrate to other countries and other societies.

Cultures cannot be excavated with ancient fossils. Stone tools, Spears, Clay pots etc are a reflection of a culture and society of the time that ancestor died. Those artifacts are a "snapshot" in time. Many Archeological finds can be discovered from an earlier cultural learning and skills.

Any group or size of group have their own cultures and traditions. Families can have their own traditions or cultures. The evolution of the human race has been reliant on these traditions and cultures. Parents have taught their children lessons that they have learned in order to survive, including lessons of danger, how to identify and avoid those dangers. Humans are not unique with this. Chimpanzee mothers teach their offspring the social rules and hierarchy within their societies. Males are taught hunting skills from the elders of the society. Females are taught how to nurse and care for their babies and patterns of behaviour, just like humans.

Petroglyphs in Azerbaijan from 10,000 years ago. Indicating a thriving culture

Every culture has their own cultural language. When people speak of German, Spanish, Japanese, Samoan etc, they are referring to the shared language, traditions and beliefs that set these societies apart from other societies.

Many fundamental elements make up a societies culture, including religion, arts, cuisine, language and history. The last two centuries have seen an influx of immigrants to other countries and societies, making many more societies "multi cultural". For instance, today's United States of America is made up of immigrants from England, Poland, Germany, Asia, Africa, mainly all contributing to today's North American culture. The main language is an American form of the English language. The main religion is Christian, The arts are primarily based on European art, as is with the American Cuisine. Dance consists of contemporary English styles, Rock N Roll, Hip Hop and a mix of African styles.

Since the first hominids migrated out of Africa, certain characteristics have changed or evolved over different regions of the World. People living in tropic and sub-tropic regions have differing colours of skin. Melanin in the skin determines the colour and genetics is responsible for varying skin colour with other variations such as, a pink tinge in skin colour can be caused by the blood vessels under the skin.

Between seventy thousand and one hundred thousand years ago. Migrating humans moved further from tropic regions. Exposing them to less severe sunlight and possibly the need for clothing to protect them from increasing cold conditions. This is believed to have caused the darker skin genes to become less dominant over time. Lighter skin was able to generate more Vitamin D than darker skin enabling the skin to become lighter.

The Earth has existed now for 4.5 billion years. The evolution of life on earth has been ongoing now for 3.5 billion years. The evolution of humans, from their earliest ancestor has now been ongoing for 8 million years. Over geological and evolutionary time, the evolution of humans has occurred over the blink of an evolutionary eye. We have built a world for ourselves, which has changed beyond recognition from our evolutionary ancestors. Our early ancestor struggled for survival, they eventually made basic tools from wood and stone. During this time, they learned to harness and control fire for warmth and heating. They migrated from their ancestral home and eventually occupied every area of the globe. Along the way, they learned how to farm and grow their own food, while creating and building bigger societies, civilizations and empires. Exploring and mapping the world

Humans have certainly changed the world, when you see where we are today. Our technology and what we can build. We have gone from the basics of technology and shelter to dominating the world and able to extend into space and other worlds. It's certainly hard to believe we are the same people that made those stone tools.

Conclusion

O ver 150 years ago in 1858, Charles Darwin published his Book, On The Origin Of species, By Means Of Natural Selection. Outlining a theory, which would become extremely debated over the years since, but would become the standard understanding of evolution of all living forms on earth today, in doing so, would become the most influential book ever written.

Charles Darwin was not the first naturalist to propose a theory of evolution. But he was the first to formulate an argument for his theory of natural selection. Containing three main parts to his theory, being: more offspring will be produced from a population that can possibly survive different environments, individual traits will vary between individuals leading to different rates of survival and reproduction and differences in any new trait will be heritable. Meaning, when members of a populations die off, they will be replaced with populations that are better adapted to survive and reproduce in changing environments.

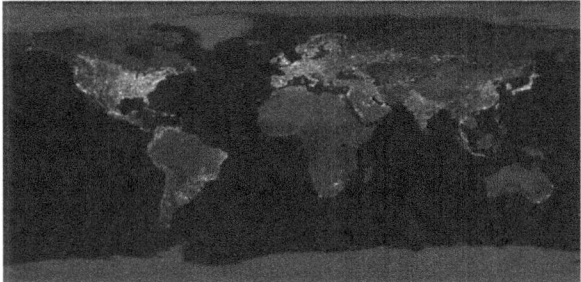

The Habitation of Humans on Earth is shown at night with the night lighting.

Evolution is no longer a theory. It is the standard model that is recognised on how all life has diversified or changed over the years. Originating from a common ancestor, diversifying into different lineages, then different species and advancing into the modern life we see all over the world today, through natural selection, favouring any genetic changes that benefit future generations for changing environments.

An inability or failure to evolve or adapt to changing environments will lead to a species extinction.

Throughout the history of life on Earth, most of the different species to have existed are now extinct. Extinction is the ultimate fate for all living creatures on Earth. Throughout Earth history, extinction events have spiked with mass extinction events. The best known of such events was the Cretaceous Mass extinction event, which saw the disappearance of the Dinosaur. The earlier Permian extinction saw the dying out of 96 percent of all living species on Earth. Undeniably, the earth is witnessing another extinction event, caused with the expansion of humans around the world.

Since the Cretaceous extinction, 65 million years ago, species have evolved, then become extinct, such as the saber toothed tiger and Mammoths have become extinct and various other less known species. By the middle of the twenty first century it is estimated that 30 percent of all animal species on earth today will become extinct. The current global change or climate warming may accelerate this extinction.

After the extinction of the Neanderthal and Denisovan species, the homo species were alone, the last hominid species on earth. Within 40 thousand years, Homo sapiens have colonised the entire world, free from any other hominid competition.

This is finally us. Physically the result of 3 million years of evolutionary change, over three hundred thousand generations since the first true human species, Australopithecus afarensis (Lucy). Eight million years since the first primate ancestor.

We are now fully human, with our large brain and in our mind. It is that which has provided us with that critical edge.

The main ability that we know that our earliest ancestor did not do, that we do well is, express ourselves artistically, the social systems, the richness of communication, both spoken languages and symbolically has made us who we are.

The same mind that has undergone so many changes and development, one day asked the obvious question. Where did we all come from?

For over the last 150 years, we have been finding the answers to that question. The evidence discovered so far has given us a clearer picture. A snap shot of our past. We have come a long way and the search has not stopped.

Uncovering our evolutionary past has been a monumental journey, but it is still not over. The specimens found so far leads to some important questions. What else is out there? What else are we going to find? Over the next few decades as scientists find other areas of the planet they have not yet examined, who knows what they are going to find.

Appreciation

I would personally like to thank you for purchasing and reading this book. I enjoyed writing **Distinctly Human: An Evolutionary Journey**. I hope it was enjoyable for you to read.

Contact The Author:
Bruce-a@brucealpine.com

More Titles From Bruce Alpine: Visit The Website:

https://brucealpine.com

Distinctly Human:
An Evolutionary Journey

Bruce Alpine

ePub ISBN: 978-1-301-20346-8
Print ISBN: 978-1-542-35279-6